A Collective Blooming

The Rise Of The Mutual Aid Community

Joe Lightfoot

Table Of Contents

An Introduction:
This Book In A Nutshell

This is a bite sized book about rediscovering each other. It explores how cultivating new types of community can bring untold fulfilment into our lives, and puts forward the idea that a globally synchronised burst of grass roots community engagement may have the potential to radically transform our inner and outer worlds.

The book is composed of four parts:

- Part I briefly explores the nature of our modern day alienation and suggests that without major structural changes our whole civilisation may soon be headed for collapse.

- Part II outlines the grand overarching narratives that helped bring us to this point, and explores some of the alternatives that are emerging in response.

- Part III introduces the idea of the Conscious Change Collective, a new form of mutual aid community that is intended to increase our felt sense of belonging, create new opportunities for us to give and receive support and empower us to become more effective agents of change. This section of the book also explores how such Collectives may be the perfect vehicles to prototype and live out the new kinds of societal narratives that are starting to emerge.

- And finally, Part IV explores the many personal benefits, challenges and opportunities that await us as individuals when we begin to participate in such mutual aid communities.

So let's begin by first taking a brief look at one of the most insidious threats that we currently face as a species, that of our gradual descent into a culture of Alienated Hyper-individuality.

I

Wicked Problems:
Our Call to Adventure

There is a pattern to the universe and everything in it, and there are knowledge systems and traditions that follow this pattern to maintain balance, to keep the temptations of narcissism in check. But recent traditions have emerged that break down creation systems like a virus, infecting complex patterns with artificial simplicity, exercising a civilising control over what some see as chaos. **Tyson Yunkaporta**[1]

1

The Age Of Alienation: Becoming Hyper-Individuals

'All of us are pretty good at carrying the secret of our own loneliness' **Carl Rogers**[2]

Somewhere along the way, we lost touch with each other. After millions of years of evolution in tight knit tribal communities, in the blink of an historical eyelid we became a society of alienated hyper-individuals. In the words of Waldo Noesta 'a society of hyper-individualists no longer functions like a single organism, but as an aggregate of parts each looking out for its own interests, cooperating only as they see fit as a means to their own private ends'.[3] In other words, a society soon destined for decline and the cracks are already showing.

In the Global North we have less close friends we can confide in and live further apart from our family members than ever before.[4,5] Our elders are left stranded in social isolation and our youth feels increasingly disconnected and alone[6]. Worst of all is that we now know such conditions are incredibly detrimental to our physical and mental health, with recent studies showing that loneliness and isolation can result in up to a 50% increase in the likelihood of a premature death.[7] From the increasing time we spend at work, to the hours spent navigating traffic in our burgeoning cities, we've engineered a system that literally drives us away from each other and towards an early grave.

The Japanese phenomena of Kodokushi illustrates just how alienated we've become. It describes an increasing trend of people dying alone and not being discovered for extended periods of time. In the year 2000, a man's corpse was found a full three years after he'd died,[8] and only then because his savings account had been automatically emptied by his bank and he could no longer cover the cost of his rent. He died alone, and had no one in his life close enough to wonder whether or not he was still alive.

Such statistics and stories illustrate that our modern way of life is slowly eroding the threads of human connection that hold us together. But we weren't always so alienated from each other, as Carl Sagan explains 'most of human history was spent in hunter-gatherer communities. And in these kinds of communities today—there aren't many of them—you find a degree of cooperativeness, an absence of alienation that is unheard of in modern society. To ignore our social heredity is a serious mistake. There is a human capacity for good-natured cooperation that is simply not encouraged in modern society. That must change.'[9] But before exploring what such change might look like, let's first take a look at what is likely to happen to our civilisation if we continue down the road we're currently on.

2

And Then It Collapsed: Civilisation As The Ultimate Pyramid Scheme

There is a growing consensus in academia that unless we make rapid, radical and far reaching changes to our way of life, then there's a good chance that at some point in the decades to come our entire civilisation may simply collapse.[10]

We not only face the prospect of climate breakdown, the threat of ongoing pandemics and the economic hardship that will follow, but also a combination of rapid biodiversity loss, increasingly vast inequalities in the distribution of wealth, widespread oppression of minority groups, rapid technological disruptions to our economic systems, the ever present threat of nuclear war and the increasing likelihood of a series of global food shortages. Just to name a few.

Though in many ways this high level of threat is nothing new, as our species has a long and colourful history of forming societal structures that have buckled under the weight of their own increasing levels of prosperity, and the complicatedness that tends to come with it. As the historian Ronald Wright explains 'Civilizations…feed on their local ecology until it is degraded, thriving only while they grow.

When they can no longer expand, they fall victim to their own success. Civilization is a pyramid scheme'.[11]

And sadly, as we continue to plunder the natural world at ever increasing rates, our current version of civilisation appears to be no different from the rest.

What's even more disconcerting is that civilisations tend to falter just as they appear most robust. As Jared Diamond notes 'One of the main lessons to be learned from the collapses of the Maya, Anasazi, Easter Islanders, and those other past societies…is that a society's steep decline may begin only a decade or two after the society reaches its peak numbers [in population], wealth, and power.'[12] Which means that in less than twenty years time, our own socio-economic system could also begin to come apart at the seams. And due to its global span, if it falls it's likely to fall very hard indeed.

Historically the survivors of such a collapse would often move along to an adjacent ecosystem and simply start over again. But now that humanity has populated the vast majority of arable land on the planet, it seems that we're finally being asked to radically change our ways. As Jeremy Lent puts it, 'we need a fundamental transformation of society encompassing virtually every aspect of the human experience: our values, our goals and our collective behaviour. If we are to succeed in sustaining civilisation, the meaning we derive from our existence must arise from our connectedness; to ourselves, to other humans, and to the entire natural world.'[13]

So if we find ourselves the inheritors of a political, economic and cultural narrative that is leading us well and truly in the wrong direction, then it appears we have little choice but to come together and collectively rewrite a more resonant human story. But how do we do this? What are the narratives that need replacing? And which new ones might be waiting to emerge?

II

Evolving Our Narrative: The Stories That Will Shape Our World

'You cannot take away someones story without giving them a new one. It is not enough to challenge an old narrative, however discredited and outdated it may be. Change happens only when you replace it with another. When we develop the right story and learn how to tell it, it will infect the minds of people across the political spectrum. Those who tell the stories run the world.'
George Monbiot[14]

3

The Grandest Tale:
Our One True Superpower

Superman has X ray vision. The Hulk, uncanny strength. And Humans, well, we have stories. And while that may sound slightly unimpressive at first, a quick look back at the history of our species illustrates the immense power of a well spun narrative.

As the historian Yuval Harari spelt out in his seminal book Sapiens, the ability to tell stories was perhaps the major catalyst in our transformation from a relatively vulnerable savannah ape into an organism that would go on to completely rewrite the rules of the food chain. Our creation of both oral and written cultures, and the cooperative team work which they enabled, unshackled us from the glacial pace of genetic evolution and propelled us into the modern age.

This ability to construct narrative is more than just a skill we've managed to master, it's become our very means of interpreting reality. Similar to our instinct for learning language, researchers have observed an almost universal inclination in children for absorbing and creating narrative. And our personal identities can be seen as the most intricate stories of all, as each of our memories, dreams, relationships and even our very sense of self are all a form of narrative, elaborate fictions that we keep telling ourselves because we believe, often subconsciously, that they are somehow in our best interest. Our political and economic beliefs, and the systems that they underpin are all equally fictitious, each ceasing to exist the minute we stop believing in them.

But whether the stories that shape our society are objectively verifiable or not is of little consequence, as what really matters is that we act as if they were true. Which means that the effective story teller is truly the most powerful agent in human society. And with the majority of the worlds population now reachable online, the power of a well spun tale is greater than ever.

So if we wish to see change in the world we need to start rewriting our cultural script, to begin constructing transformational new narratives that appeal to our noblest selves and encourage us to keep our more selfish desires in check. As Terrence McKenna put it, 'if you're not the hero of your own novel, then what kind of novel is it? You need to do some heavy editing.' [15] And right now, in regards to acting as custodians that maintain the conditions for complex life to flourish on Earth, our modern culture is far more villainous than it is heroic.

But before we can rewrite our collective script, we first need to get clear on exactly which narratives are currently playing out. As while the grand stories of the day underpin virtually every aspect of our modern lives, they can often hide in plain sight, behind a veneer of what is generally considered as either 'accepted truth' or 'common sense'. We tend to have a blindspot regarding the baseline assumptions of our mother culture, which can make it challenging for us to conceive of wholly new ways of living, especially when all we're familiar with are the narratives with which we were raised. So before exploring some of the promising new stories that are starting to emerge, let's first gain a deeper understanding of the narratives that brought us to where we are today.

4

The Last Gasps Of Neoliberalism

For over thirty years Neoliberalism has been the dominant cultural narrative of modern society. In theory, it's a story that places a huge amount of confidence in the unrestrained market economy to decide what is good and right. In practice, it's a narrative that has generated an extraordinary amount of wealth for a very small percentage of people and done extensive damage to the underlying health of our societies and ecosystems in the process.

As Noam Chomsky said of Neoliberalism, 'instead of citizens, it produces consumers. Instead of communities, it produces shopping malls. The net result is an atomised society of disengaged individuals who feel demoralised and socially powerless. In sum, neoliberalism is the immediate and foremost enemy of genuine participatory democracy, not just in the United States, but across the planet'.[16]

It's a set of ideas that went mainstream after the elections of Margaret Thatcher and Ronald Reagan in the late 1970's. Thatcher herself might have best summed up the whole Neoliberal story line with her famous proclamation that, 'there's no such thing as society'[17], implying that we're simply a competing mass of self interested individuals inherently devoid of a social conscience. The waves of deregulation and privatisation that followed in the wake of the Neoliberal agenda led to a huge shift in responsibility away from governments and towards the private sector. Gigantic multinational corporations became increasingly effective at utilising their extraordinary wealth and lobbying power to directly influence political decisions. Which meant that the maximisation of shareholder returns remained a much higher priority than the protection of our human rights, or the safeguarding of the integrity of our democratic processes.

This led to increasingly grotesque disparities between the worlds rich and poor, to widespread exploitation of many in the Global South and enabled the war mongering Military-Industrial complex to grow ever more entrenched and influential in the halls of power. It also ensured that the corporate sector was never held accountable for the trillions of dollars of damage they had done to the worlds ecological commons. And yet just when Neoliberalism appeared to have well and truly established itself as the dominant narrative of the early 21st Century, the 2008 financial crisis saw it begin to come apart at the seams.

After the collapse of a series of the worlds largest and most trusted financial institutions, rather than attempting to remedy the underlying issues, world leaders at the time chose to simply charge head on, bailing out the banks and transferring the costs and hardships of the crisis directly to the taxpayer. It was essentially the most expensive attempt at sweeping a problem under the rug that the world had ever seen. But the bailouts did just enough to keep the the Neoliberal agenda staggering along for a few years more, before the anger, fear and hardship felt by the working classes manifested itself in 2016, first with the Brexit vote, then with the election of Donald Trump and a wave of authoritarian leaders gaining office around the world.

The winds were starting to change, a new narrative was in the ascendant, Nationalist Populism was resurfacing once more and it wasn't afraid to make a brash and garish entrance.

5

Flirting With The F Word: The Radical Populist Resurgence

Suddenly the politicians were yelling again. A new wave of 'strong men' had emerged and sensing weakness in the Neoliberal world order they pounced on the opportunity to cast themselves as heroes of the people. They forcefully declared their intentions to bring down the corrupt 'Global Elite' and were swiftly voted into power all over the world. A new story of Nationalist Populism was taking hold and promised to return our nations to their mythological states of former glory.

But as Yanis Varoufakis, the ex finance minister of Greece points out, this new wave of Populism 'has nothing to do with being popular, it's got to do with speaking in a language that exploits the fears of the disposed, in order to harness their anger, and then use it in order to usurp power for yourself.'[18] It's a new version of a story we've seen many times before.

And at this point in history it appears to prudent to ask ourselves whether or not we are witnessing the emergence of a kind of proto-fascism. In 1974, Primo Levi wrote, 'there are many ways of reaching [fascism], not just through the terror of police intimidation, but by denying and distorting information, by undermining systems of justice, by paralysing the education system, and by spreading in a myriad subtle ways nostalgia for a world where order reigned, and where the security of a privileged few depends on the forced labor and the forced silence of the many.'[19]

The recent rise of Nationalist Populism has seen the general tone of political rhetoric become markedly more aggressive and insular, with many of the dynamics Levi points to appearing worryingly apparent in the world we live in today. And while we are yet to see exactly what impact the COVID 19 pandemic will have upon the broader political landscape, it's clear that the ongoing threat of contagious disease will provide ample opportunity for those in power to further curtail our civil liberties in the name of maintaining social stability and order.

Meanwhile, despite all the nationalistic talk of making our nations great again the wars rage on, ecological destruction continues unabated, and the rich continue to profit while those at the bottom of the pyramid suffer lives of quiet indignity. It seems to be business as usual since the Populists took power, which gives credence to Frank Zappa's idea that politics as we know it is merely 'the entertainment division of the Military-Industrial complex'.[20] Indeed the whole transition from Neoliberalism towards Nationalist Populism seems to be a somewhat surface level of transformation, as both narratives appear to be symptoms of an even deeper story that seems to be growing more dominant all the time. And although this story often lurks below the

surface, largely unseen, I believe it to be the real spectre
of our age.

6

What Lies Beneath: The Hungry Ghosts Of Hollow Materialism

While there are a vast range of competing narratives currently playing out across human society, it appears to me that the most pervasive and influential of them all is a kind of Hollow & Oppressive Economic Materialism (HOEM). It's an ideology that exults the accumulation of material wealth above all other pursuits, and ascribes status to people based on what they own, rather than the quality of their actions and character. It's 'hollow' in that it creates an endless longing for more that can never be fulfilled through its own means. It's 'oppressive' in that it cares little for equity, justice or the rights of the downtrodden. It's 'economic' because it's firmly rooted in notions of who owns what. And it's 'materialistic' in that it places little worth on anything that cannot be physically grasped by acquisitive hands.

Since we first started building civilisations the HOEM narrative has been seeping ever more deeply into our collective cultural code. Over the last two thousand years it has come to wholly subsume the intricate egalitarian ethic we spent millennia cultivating together as hunter gatherers, replacing it instead with a series of interlinking dominator hierarchies that leave us constantly pitted against one another and always at war.

The HOEM narrative thrived in the wake of the Enlightenment, finding fertile soil in a culture that had proclaimed God dead, where scientific rationality and mass industrialisation were on the ascendent. It then produced a series of patriarchal and systemically racist socio-economic systems that were forcefully promulgated around the world by colonial imperialism, resulting in the emergence of an ecologically and socially corrosive global plutocracy which continues to profit from the subjugation of countless oppressed peoples to this very day. As the author John Perkins spells out it's a paradigm driven forward, 'by a concept that has become accepted as gospel: the idea that all economic growth benefits humankind and that the greater the growth, the more widespread the benefits. This belief also has a corollary: that those people who excel at stoking the fires of economic growth should be exalted and rewarded, while those born at the fringes are available for exploitation.' [21]

In more recent times the HOEM narrative appears to have finally reached its apex, manifesting in the form of a rampant global consumerism that effortlessly transcends national borders and quickly co-opts any culture it encounters. As early as the 1970's the economist Tibor Schitovsky labelled such a paradigm the Joyless Economy, as while it has resulted in many people experiencing higher standards of material comfort, it has stripped much of the joy out of many peoples lived experience of day to day life. In a tragic twist of irony this pervasive misery even encompasses those who appear to benefit most from the status quo, with recent research showing that higher income levels don't equate to higher life satisfaction and that the more materialistic individuals amongst us tend to experience lower levels of well-being.[22]

Like all grand narratives, HOEM comes complete with its very own set of underlying beliefs, which tend to run on endless repeat in the recesses of the modern mind. They include ideas that we must:

- **Accumulate More** - Be it a bigger house, a newer car, a better phone. We are programmed to believe that we never have enough and are entitled to more no matter the cost.

- **Become More Attractive** - The media, entertainment and advertising industries are constantly reinforcing the idea that we are not ok the way we are, and that we must become more attractive in order to feel whole.

- **Achieve At All Costs** - You are not worthy of being loved and respected until you achieve widespread notoriety. You will only feel truly complete once you become famous and rich.

Operating along side these beliefs are a series of assumptions that the majority of us in modern society seem to be culturally indoctrinated with as children. They include the ideas that:

- **It's A Jungle Out There** - Life is a thankless battle for limited resources, there isn't enough food, love or attention to satisfy everyones basic needs.

- **Look Out For Number One** - Selfishness is rational, and rationality is everything, therefore selfishness is everything.[23] As such it always makes sense to put our individual desires before the collective wellbeing.

- **Do Not Trust The Other** - People who look, sound or act differently to the 'cultural mainstream' should be feared, treated with suspicion and never be allowed to gain too much power.

- **Humans Are Inherently Separate From Nature** - Thus we are entitled to complete dominion over the rest of the natural world, and that the animal kingdom exists to be exploited however we wish.

- **Death Is Taboo** - It should be feared and hidden away. It is best not thought about, let alone celebrated as part of the mystery of existence.

Over time this collection of beliefs and assumptions has driven us further away from each other and towards the comfortable numbness of our increasingly isolated and digital worlds. These ideas act as self replicating mind viruses that further perpetuate themselves by compelling us to try and fill the emotional black holes they create within us with even greater levels of material security and success.

And as the work of the theorist Theodor Adorno explores, they are a part of a narrative that is difficult to ever overthrow as it is continually reenforced by a cultural industry and entertainment machine that keeps us distracted, pliant and intimidated whilst simultaneously draining our will to alter the status quo.

So if the hungry ghosts of Hollow Oppressive Economic Materialism grow ever more prevalent by the day, where are they leading us? What kind of future lies in store for a society helplessly addicted to a never ever ending buffet of technologically fuelled consumption? What strange dystopia might we be in the process of birthing?

7

The Age Of Algorithms:
A Transhumanist's Wet Dream

The Age of Algorithms is upon us. A time of artificial intelligence, automated industry and driverless vehicles. A world in which data is the new currency and where the algorithms tracking our lifestyle choices may soon come to know us better than we know ourselves. But as our applied ethics continue to lag further and further behind the breakneck pace of technological development, it's a time when many of us will soon be left to grapple with the stark realisation that we've become essentially superfluous components in an increasingly faceless and technical economic system.

Looming alongside the prospect of such a heavily centralised algorithmic future, is the emerging Transhumanist narrative. It envisages an ongoing blend of man and machine until the two become indistinguishable, promising advanced genetic engineering, direct brain to computer interfaces, extended lifespans and freedom from the shackles of all of our biological limitations. However, without a radical shift in the way power and wealth is shared throughout society, such developments may only result in the bifurcation of humanity into new genetic castes. As the biologist Lee Silver warns, if we allow only the wealthiest amongst us to access such technologies, then over time the haves and have nots within society may become soon entirely separate species, at some point accruing so much genetic difference that they lose romantic interest in each other and no longer choose to procreate.[24]

While dazzling us with promises of a kind of techno utopia, I often find that such cornucopian visions of the future fail to meaningfully engage with the political, social and environmental issues that already threaten our survival as a species. In many ways, such narratives are really just accelerated versions of the Hollow Oppressive Economic Materialism we already have today. It's my belief that if we continue on with business as usual, blindly rushing into an increasingly technological age, then it will become even easier for the small number of individuals who already own the lions share of the worlds intellectual property to control even wider tracts of society. Which means that if the rest of us become distracted by increasingly intoxicating and addictive virtual worlds, then we face the very real prospect of waking up one day to discover that increasingly draconian forms of Digital Authoritarianism have curtailed our rights and usurped our freedoms.

And yet, there is hope. As outside of the mainstream media, a new consensus is beginning to emerge. And although each of the individual narratives it's comprised of have their own distinct flavour, when overlaid on one another they create the outlines of a markedly more egalitarian and inspiring future for our species. Let's take a look now at the kinds of narratives that are pointing towards a new era of compassionate togetherness.

8

A Time Of Togetherness:
An Emergent Consensus

There is an alternative consensus emerging with many philosophers, economists and social theorists all arriving at a very similar conclusion. Essentially that we need to embrace an entirely new narrative based on the overarching principle of compassionate togetherness and then reengineer our society from the ground up. Here is just a small selection (in alphabetical order) of some of the many new narratives emerging:

- The Commons Economy & P2P Culture - Michel Bauwens & The P2P Foundation

- Communalism & Social Ecology - Murray Bookchin

- The Emergence Of Regenerative Culture - Magenta Ceiba & The Bloom Network. As well as Daniel Christian Wahl.

- The Progressive International - Ada Colau, Bernie Sanders, Yanis Varakoulous & Cornel West.

- The Mythology of Interbeing - Charles Eiesenstein & Thich Nhat Hanh

- The Listening Society & Metamodernism - Hanzi Frienhacht.

- The Great Turning - Joanna Macy.

26

- The New Human Rights Movement & The Resource Based Economy - Peter Joseph & TZM.

- A Politics Of Belonging - George Monbiot.

- Local Futures: An Economics Of Happiness - Helena Norberg-Hodge.

- Earth Democracy & Seeding A Common Future - Vandana Shiva.

- The Extinction Rebellion & Climate Activists such as Greta Thunberg.

- And while each of the following thinkers might be sagely skeptical of the notion of any new overarching narratives, it feels important to me to presence the work of Bayo Akomolafe, Angela Davis and Tyson Yunkaporta. As the elements of mythopoetry, critical analysis and Indigenous wisdom they offer up are perhaps some of the most crucial pieces of any kind of regenerative culture that may emerge in the years to come.

Each of the narratives listed above proposes a unique approach to reforming our social, economic and political systems, however they all share a similar set of underlying values and they all point towards a a future that is:

- Regenerative
- Collaborative
- Community Based
- Networked
- Planetary In Scope
- Interdependent

- Empathic
- Pluralist
- Integrative
- Anti Rivalrous
- Participatory
- Peer to Peer
- Open Source

I like to think of this emerging vision for the future of our society as being a kind of Compassionate Global Village. And in the name of a healthy, diverse and yet philosophically aligned collection of new narratives that might help realise such a world, I'd now like to introduce one more, A Collective Blooming.

9

A Collective Blooming: Towards The Compassionate Global Village

A Collective Blooming is a narrative that revolves around the cultivation of community. It envisions a planet wide network of peaceful, cooperative, decentralised, ecologically sustainable and socially just local communities. Essentially a worldwide transition from the corrosive, hollow, oppressive & materialistic plutocracy we have today, towards the regenerative, enlightened & compassionate global village that is already starting to emerge in small pockets all over the world. It's a narrative that points toward a society where all living beings on Earth are afforded lives of dignity and where the health of our inner worlds, our relationships and our communal bonds are all placed at the heart of our cultural and political agenda.

The Collective Blooming narrative can be visualised as a global ecosystem of change making collectives all coming into blossom at precisely the same moment, a kind of floral chain of empathic, community focused activation that unites those of us ready and willing to step into the next chapter of our development as a species. It's an invitation for us to start co-creating the world we wish to live in, right here in the world we inhabit today. Admittedly, it's a fairly idealistic vision. But as we find ourselves facing a number of existential crises, it seems

---

we have no other choice but to remain focussed on the vision of a better world and then keep moving towards it, one courageous step at a time.

Part of this process is to continually remind ourselves that the future is what we choose to make it. As the author Richard Flanagan put it, 'perhaps the greatest problem we face is not climate change, but the myth of our own powerlessness. We believe only the most powerful – the politicians, the corporations – can change our world. Accordingly, we feel a great despair about our future because we can see no hope in any politician or any corporation. But it is not so. Because the only thing that will save us is us. Half of the carbon in the atmosphere was put there by us in the last 30 years. And now we have eleven and a half years to reverse that disastrous act. It is a time to act and it is for us to act. Because there is no one else and there is no other time.'[25]

And whilst we must respond urgently to the wide range of environmental catastrophes and social injustices that face our species, the longer journey towards any such Compassionate Global Village will be a multi generational effort. It will take time, patience and an appetite for experimenting with radically new ways of living. But if we remain alienated and left to feel alone in the face of such massive existential threats, then the challenges before us can begin to appear almost insurmountable.

Which is why I believe one of the first and most important steps we can take is to more fully harness the power of community. To foster the kind of human scaled cultural ecosystems that allow us to weave our lives together in ways that encourage us to heal, blossom and then work together towards enacting sustained waves of social, political and economic change.

In modern society the true value of community is often grossly underestimated. But in my experience it's one of the most powerful tools that we have, as in just a matter of months it can completely transform an individuals life and empower them to become much more effective agents of change. But to access this transformational power we must first generate a new wave of mutual aid communities that are well adapted to the 21st Century, that serve to connect, nurture, unite and inspire all those individuals with their sights firmly set on a better tomorrow.

So if cultivating new kinds of community is one of the quickest routes to the Compassionate Global Village, then let's now explore what kind of vehicles might be best suited to take us on such a journey.

III

Imagining The Conscious Change Collective

'Never doubt that a small group of thoughtful, committed citizens can change the world; indeed, it's the only thing that ever has.' **Margaret Mead**[26]

10

The Story Of Us:
A Thought Experiment

Imagine we're part of a small group of five people who don't yet know one another, but are about to become a very important part of each others lives. Imagine that we begin to each cross paths with one another, meeting at workshops, whole food cafes, co-working spaces and other kinds of events. Imagine that we immediately recognise the same hopes, dreams and sorrows shining in each others eyes.

The five of us begin to hang out and get to know each other more deeply, sharing meals, spending time in nature and making music with each other. We put words to the sadness that each of us feel in relation to all the suffering we see in the world, and we learn that despite our sorrow, each one of us remains steadfastly committed to doing whatever we can to make the world a better place. We discover a shared intention for personal growth, for making change in the world and for having as much fun as possible while we do it.

And before long these intentions form the basis of a potent communal bond. We discover that just by spending time together we pollinate one another with new insights and ideas. We laugh, dance, cry and shout together at the top of our lungs. We remind one another that we're alive, and that while our hearts are still beating there is always hope for a better tomorrow. We start to feel a sense of being at home when we are in each others company.

Over time each of us invites in other friends that also wish to share in the experience. And as our shared connections deepen, we begin to practice relating authentically and compassionately with one another. We form small groups we call Pods and hold space for each other to share about the intimacies of our inner experiences. We open up about the more challenging emotions many of us experience in our day to day lives and begin to celebrate each others victories. We articulate, capture and share our personal dreams with one another and when invited to, we hold each other accountable in following through with our commitments towards making such dreams a reality. Little by little, as we share more of our personal stories, we begin to open up and trust each other enough to talk about our vulnerabilities and insecurities. We begin to let down some of our emotional armour.

Some of us choose to go deeper with this process, actively supporting each other to bring awareness and acceptance to those parts of ourselves we've had a tendency to avoid or repress. We discover that deep in our hearts each one of us has been carrying around an unexpressed reservoir of aloneness, a yearning to be seen and appreciated for who we feel we really are. We learn that we all share a common desire to drop the masks that we so often find ourselves wearing and that every one of us has been actively seeking out a lived experience of the full spectrum of physical, emotional, intellectual and spiritual human connection. A state of being and a way of relating that deep down we've always known to be possible.

And before long, we decide to formalise our organic network of relationships in the hope that it will help to strengthen our new found sense of community and ensure that it remains healthy and resilient over time. After a few whole group meetings to fully explore the idea, we all agree to form a new mutual aid community, and so our Collective is born. The twenty or so people that form the group all come from many different walks of life, but we each hold a similar vision for the future and have agreed upon a shared set of values and guidelines for the how the Collective will operate.

We start to gather out of town once or twice a year, spending three or four days just being in each others company, away from the hustle and bustle of daily life. Many of us meet regularly each week and help one another with the projects that are important to us, sharing support, expertise and advice wherever it's welcomed. Some of us co-create events, others collaborate on business ventures and social enterprises and a few of the freelancers in the group experiment with pooling their income streams together. When tensions arise, we do our best to clash gracefully and encourage conflict resolution whenever there are major disagreements and fallouts. And all the while we remain ever vigilant of the kinds of unhealthy group dynamics that can so often emerge in such close communal contexts.

Along the way we continually educate and update each other about the causes that are most dear to our heart's. We playfully inspire one another to start integrating more social and ecological awareness into our lifestyle choices. We regularly grieve together about the injustice we see in the world and attempt to make sense of what appears to be an increasingly uncertain future. We raise money together for causes we believe in and reconnect to our local food sources, supporting and becoming involved with nearby organic farms and permaculture centres. We plan for how we can adapt to the environmental and social changes looming on our horizon and strive to determine how best our Collective can offer up support to the wider community around us. We engage in activism work together, continually motivating and empowering each other to become ever more effective advocates of political and social change.

And one day, we each awake to the realisation that we've collectively woven a thriving trust network from which we all draw a strong sense of belonging, support and shared purpose. It dawns on us that we've cultivated our very own pocket of regenerative culture, and that each of us feels an integral part of its creation. We discover that without having jeopardised our own personal sense of freedom, privacy or individuality, we've become deeply engrained in a human container that encourages and empowers us to enact positive change in our selves and the world. We've found loving community and surrounded ourselves with the kind of people we wish to grow along side of throughout our journey through life.

*　*　*

This story depicts the formation of a Conscious Change Collective, a new type of mutual aid community that may be able to help us collectively bloom in the decades ahead. Let's now explore exactly what these Collectives are, how they might improve our lives and how they might hasten our transition into a whole new narrative.

11

Find The Others: Start A Collective

Conscious Change Collectives (which I'll just refer to as Collectives from here on in) are a new form of mutual aid community, made up of anywhere between 15-250 people that all wish to share a deep sense of communal belonging with one another. The central idea is to form a trust network of relationships with a group of people that all share the same core values and then to cultivate as many opportunities as possible to share meaningful experiences with one another, to grow and evolve as individuals and to work together to bring about radical and positive change across wider society. Collectives are designed to be incubators for the creation of a whole new type of regenerative culture. They are 'Conscious' because a central part of the experience is about becoming more consciously aware of how we relate to our ourselves and each other. And they are 'Change' focused in that beyond the experience of cultivating a deep sense of solidarity with one another, such communities are intended to help us actively transform our societal model.

In essence, Collectives provide us with a direct experience of just how nurturing it can be to co-create a thriving sense of community with a group of people with whom we feel we belong. They are are intended to empower us to become more integrated versions of ourselves, whilst simultaneously increasing our effectiveness as agents of social change. And they do this by serving as active invitations for us to continually step into seven different types of practice:

1. **Waking Up** - Becoming acutely aware of the extraordinary suffering and injustice that is occurring on our planet and gaining a comprehensive understanding of the various existential crises we now face as a species. Waking Up also involves continually educating ourselves around how best to make a difference.

2. **Tuning In** - Tapping into the subtle and spiritual (à la the Metamoderna interpretation) aspects of our own inner experiences. Feeling more deeply into the changing states of our bodies and minds through contemplative, meditative and mindfulness based practices.

3. **Leaning In** - Having the courage to show up in community, to engage with others and take on a level of responsibility within the group. To open our hearts and risk having them touched by those around us.

4. **Integrating In** - Recognising those areas in which we still need to mature and grow. Identifying our own interpersonal edges and personal trauma and then doing the work to integrate those parts of our selves we are either not yet conscious of or have perhaps chosen to repress.

5. **Levelling Up** - Recognising the kind of cultural codes and cognitive frames we use to interpret the world and continually orienting ourselves towards a more nuanced and all encompassing understanding of how the world works and our place within it.[27]

---

6. **Throwing Down** - Directing our energies towards making art, music or any other kind of creative endeavour that allows us to fully express ourselves and share the fruit of our talents with our wider community.

7. **Giving Back** - Taking effective action towards bringing about more ecological balance, social justice, peace and joyfulness into the world.

On a day to day basis this takes the form of a diverse group of people regularly partaking in a wide range of activities and experiences together. Such activities may include, but are by no means limited to:

- Annual Gatherings & Retreats.
- Book Clubs, Study Groups & Philosophy Nights.
- Celebrations, Festivities & Parties.
- Circling Pods (A form of peer to peer group therapy).
- Co-Working Sessions.
- Documentary & Movie Nights.
- Fundraising efforts for social and environmental causes.
- Goal Setting & Accountability Groups.
- Group Activism Work (Conservation, Social Justice, Animal Rights etc.).
- Kids Activities - Playtimes, Adventures & Workshops.
- Life Drawing & Creative Arts Sessions.
- Musical Jam Nights, Dance Events & Performances.
- Open Mic Nights & Poetry Nights.

- Online Forums & Social Media Groups.
- Permaculture & Community Gardening Days.
- Personal Sustainability Audits & Challenges.
- Physical Training, Sports, Acrobatics & Treks.
- Plant Medicine Ceremonies & Breath work Sessions.
- Political Actions (Campaigning, Marches & Occupations).
- Potluck Dinners & Shared Meals.
- Rewilding Practices.
- Skill Shares (Cooking, Gardening, Massage, Martial arts etc.).
- Speakers & Group Discussion Nights.
- Social Enterprise Incubators.
- Womens & Mens Groups.
- Yoga & Meditation Sessions.

While these kinds of activities form the backbone of the Collective experience, participating in such a community is as much about being as it is about doing. As underneath the veneer of our increasingly technological lives we remain social primates at heart, biologically and psychologically inclined to spend large amounts of time simply relishing in each others company. And this is one of central aspects of the Collective experience, remembering how to become quietly and deeply comfortable in one another's shared presence. Two of the more central activities that allow us to do this, are the holding of Gatherings and the forming of Pods.

Gatherings are multi-day events that are held by a Collective around once or twice a year. They might best be described as part celebration, part conference and part retreat. They are a chance for everyone in the community to come together and spend time exclusively in each others company. They help us to renew the bonds of understanding and belonging that bind our communities together and provide us with the opportunity to experience peak moments of connection with one another. They are also a way for new people to connect in with the culture of a Collective and decide if they would like to become more deeply involved.

Pods are small groups that form within a Collective in order to share in a particular type of experience together. They can be conducted in person or online and come in many shapes and sizes, but they tend to be most effective when they are made up of between 3-6 people. Depending upon the needs and wishes of the particular Pod, they can happen over a period of weeks, months or go on indefinitely. They can take many different forms but here is a list of some of the more common examples:

- **Circling Pods** - A form of peer to peer group therapy, where participants regularly come together to share about their inner experiences and gain a deeper understanding of each others internal worlds. Some of these Circling Pods may be open to all members of the Collective and others may be focused on certain demographics within the group, such as BIPOC or LGQBT+ folks.
- **Learning Pods** - A group of people that come together to study a certain course, subject or approach to personal development.

- **Enterprise & Project Pods** - A group of people that either directly undertake a new project or social enterprise together, or else support one other in kickstarting or further developing projects or businesses they are already running on their own.

- **Goals & Accountability Pod** - A group of people that come together to set personal goals and then support each other to stay accountable in moving towards them.

- **Skill Share Pods** - A group of people that take turns in teaching each other particular skills or expertise.

- **Activism Pods** - A group of people dedicated to educating themselves and then taking action towards progressing a particular cause.

There are countless different ways that Pods of people can come together to support and empower each other, and the intimacy and depth they allow for is one of the backbones of the whole Collective experience. Beyond the holding of Gatherings and the formation of Pods, there are two other central components which help to lay the foundations for a Collective to flourish.

The first of these is an online platform where people in the community can stay connected and in touch with each other no matter where they are in the world. Secondly, the right collection of online tools can empower a Collective to make more effective decisions as a group and allow all sorts creative and project based collaboration to unfold. The final component is a physical space, or even a series of them, where people in the Collective can regularly meet up and partake in the various kinds of activities listed above. This can take the form of a co-working space, a cafe or even someones private home.

So, to recap, the minimum viable structure for a Collective to blossom includes:

- A group of people who all share the same values as well as a desire to cultivate a strong sense of communal belonging.
- The holding of annual in person Gatherings.
- An ongoing cycle of Pods.
- An online platform on which to connect and collaborate and if possible a physical space where everyone can regularly cross paths in person.

So if that's a broad overview of what Collectives are, let's now take a look at the many ways they can enrich our lives.

12

Coming Home: The Many Benefits Of Getting Collective

There are many benefits to participating in 'true community', which the author M. Scott Peck defined as being 'a group of individuals who have learned how to communicate honestly with each other, whose relationships go deeper than their masks of composure, and who have developed some significant commitment to rejoice together, mourn together, and to delight in each other, to make others conditions their own.'[28] Such community can bring untold levels of joy, support and belonging into our lives. It can expose us to new ideas and perspectives, encourage us to nurture our innate gifts and create opportunities for us to be seen in our totality. But other than living out the experience ourselves, perhaps the best way to gain an understanding of the deeply nourishing sense of wholeness that joining such communities can offer us, is to hear directly from those who have experienced it themselves.

Here are some personal reflections from friends of mine that have participated in Collective like contexts:

'Everyone is so magnificently different. There are artists, teachers, breath workers, hypnotherapists, singers, actors, comedians, website builders, musicians, authors, block chain experts, mud and earth builders, therapists, yogis, digital nomads, clowns, coders, painters, flow artists, tattoo artists, magicians and DJ's. Some are in their late teens or early 20s, some in their 60s, and even 70s, and everywhere in between. Everyone is so unique. But the magic lies in how each of us, in all of our uniqueness, keeps learning from each other, keeps sharing our skills and continually supporting one another. Our differences are what bring us together and inspire us to keep growing.'

'This is home, love, support and family. I've been wandering around looking for a miracle to belong to. And after finding it my life has changed in so many beautiful and empowering ways that seemed impossible to reach at first. I've reached many dreams with this community and found new family that holds my hand and allows me to step in their footprints in order to reach my goals and wishes. Mindfulness is key here. Everyday I'm reminding myself of how lucky I am to live this life with these beautiful humans and their creations. Here is the perfect place to express yourself the way you truly are and wish to be. Music, art, words, dances, hugs, appreciation, mindfulness. It allows you to nourish the flower of love within you, and it blossoms to eternity. It makes you feel comfortable within yourself. Makes you feel at home.'

Beyond empowering us to transform our own individual lives, Collectives can also act as vehicles for us to reinvigorate and renew our political and economic systems. They provide us with a chance to experiment with new social technologies such as Sociocracy, Nonviolent Communication, Gift Economics and

Restorative Justice. And by exposing us to new ways of peacefully organising ourselves, participating in Collectives can also empower us to become more politically effective citizens.

As Noam Chomsky put it, 'if a real democracy is going to thrive, if the real values that are deeply embedded in human nature are going to flourish, and I think that's necessary to save us if nothing else, I think its an absolute necessity that groups form, in which people can join together, can share their concerns, can articulate their ideas, can gain a response, can discover what they think, can discover what they believe, what their values are. This can't be imposed on you from above, you have to discover it. By experiment, by effort, by trial, by application and so on, and this has to be done with others, furthermore central to human nature is a need to be engaged with others in cooperative efforts of solidarity and concern. That can only happen by definition through group structures... There are all kinds of ways in which people can associate with each other, and what I would like to see is a move towards a society which is really based on proliferating voluntary organisation, which eliminate as much as possible the structures of hierarchy and domination... (and for such voluntary organisations) to become the means by which we govern ourselves, by which we control our lives.'[29]

Seeing as he first shared these words in 1988, it's clear that the idea of coming together and forming such transformational community groups has been around for a long time. The real question then is why hasn't it happened on a larger scale already? And what might make the years ahead any different? Let's now explore why the 2020's may be the decade when we are vehemently compelled to rediscover each other and Collectively Bloom.

13

The 2020's: A Perfect Storm For A Collective Emergence

From our time together in hunter gatherer tribes, to our more contemporary experiments in establishing Citizens Assemblies, Communes and Eco Villages, our species has a long history of forming Collective like structures. And this trend continues today, with a whole new wave of mutual aid communities now beginning to take shape all over the world, especially in response to the COVID-19 pandemic, which has served as a stark reminder of just how valuable local trust networks can be in times of need. And it seems as if in the decade ahead, this trend will only grow stronger, with the conditions appearing just right for a kind of perfect storm of collective emergence. Let's take a look now at some of the factors that are leading us away from the status quo, and towards a whole new way of interrelating.

The Factors Moving Us Away
From The Old Story

- **We're Alienated** - With increasingly high levels of loneliness & isolation being experienced throughout modern society.

- **We're Stressed** - We work long hours and often lack the time, energy and context to cultivate a variety of

deep and meaningful human relationships in our
lives.

- **We're Separated From The Wilderness** - Many of
us lack exposure to the healing effects of spending
time in wholly natural environments.

- **We're Afraid** - We face the prospect of our
environmental and social issues getting much worse
before they get better.

- **We're Angry** - We're enraged by the inequality and
injustice in our system and the ever increasing
disparities in levels of wealth and income.

- **We're Disconnected** - We're now experiencing the
delocalisation and depersonalisation that has resulted
from over three decades of rapid globalisation.

- **We're Skeptical** - With many of us having lost trust
in our major institutions.

The Factors That Are Empowering Us To Form New Kinds Of Mutual Aid Community

- **We're Motivated** - As we come to terms with the
challenges on our horizon, many of us are
experiencing a strong desire to explore new of ways
of living and working together.

- **We're Networked** - We have an increased ability to
communicate and collaborate across new online
platforms.

- **We're Equipped** - We have access to new
technologies such as 3D printers, small scale
renewable energy systems and blockchains, each of
which increases our level of community autonomy

by allowing us to further decentralise the means of production.

- **We're Mobile** - With more people freelancing and working remotely, we have more flexibility in where we choose to live and how we spend our time.

So if this gives us a better understanding of why mutual aid communities may soon start to emerge in much greater numbers. Let's now explore which kinds of people are showing up as the early adopters.

14

The Who: Not Just For Millennials

Collectives tend to attract people of all ages, with each generation being drawn towards the experience for slightly different reasons:

- **Gen Z** (born between 1995-2020) because they are the youngest adults amongst us and are naturally drawn to projects that challenge the status quo and push the boundaries of what was previously considered possible. Many of them are also digital natives that have a global perspective and a clear sense of how quickly we can make use of new social networks to effect change in our technological age.

- **Millennials** (born between 1980-1995) because they are the first generation that has had no choice but to squarely face up to the fact that our species is facing total Climate Breakdown. They are also well aware that they will face the consequences of such ecological catastrophe in their lifetimes and because of this, they don't just desire change, they recognise that it's our only hope for survival.

- **Generations X** (born between 1965-1980) because after living through three decades of intensely Hollow & Oppressive Economic Materialism, many of them harbour a kind of pragmatic resilience that is coupled with a deep yearning to pass a more resonant and meaningful societal model onto their children.

- **Baby Boomers** (born between 1945-65) because they are now of retiring age and have more time available to engage with causes they believe in. A lot of Boomers are also lucky enough to still remember the high water mark of the late sixties and so have a living memory of what can happen when a large movement of people begin to mobilise towards creating a better world. Many Boomers also have much hard earned wisdom they wish to share and are attracted to the idea of having a caring communal support network around them as they age.

The Quadruple H Population

But no matter their generation, anyone wishing to participate in prototyping such new forms of mutual aid community will have to be a courageous, patient and open hearted individual. The early adopters are likely to have a strong commitment to social justice, creative expression and personal growth. And there is a good chance that many of them (but by no means all) will be composed of a demographic that the author Hanzi Frienacht has described as the Quadruple H Population. That of Hippies, Hipsters, Hackers and Hermetics. In Hanzi's words:'A hacker is not just a person who illegally gains access to computer systems; the hackers I refer to, self-identified…or not…produce digital solutions and software that reduce the complexity of society and make it manageable. Of course, not all IT-workers, computer engineers and programmers can be considered to be hackers in this sense. Only the ones who *combine* their IT and programming skills with an intimate, embodied knowledge of digital culture (and other sensitivities towards our day and age) can be considered as such....

Hipsters are not just people with a particular style of fashion, or the pretentious college kids who show off their supposedly good taste in music and art. The hipsters I refer to produce the many symbols that help us to orientate ourselves in, make sense of, and find meaning in the global, digital age. Here you find a wide array of artists, designers, thinkers, social entrepreneurs, writers and bloggers. They develop the ideas of posthumanism, transhumanism, complexity and network researchers, participatory forms of politics and social movements, critique of wage labor (and the often irrational nature of work in the economy), ecological and social resilience, personal development, organizational development, the new gender and sexual relations, our forms of family and community life, the interactions of different cultures – and much more. They also, notably, *embody* these new thoughts by creating music, fashion, movies, books and games that embody these new values and ideas....

The Hippies are the people who produce new lifestyles, habits and practices that make life in postindustrial society happier, healthier and, perhaps, more enchanted. The hippies here are not quite the same as the hippies of old: the starry-eyed New Agers who looked to astrology, crystals, transpersonal psychologies and gurus, but rather people with highly developed skills in meditation, contemplation, bodily practices, psychedelics, diets and physical training, profound forms of intimate communication and sexuality and simple life wisdoms that apply to our day and age.'[30] Hanzi has recently added a fourth category, that of the Hermetics. He describes them as being primarily focused on the kinds of 'transrational' truths that are often approached through the study of comparative religion, archetypal forms, symbolic patterns and cross cultural mythology. Hermetics seek to bridge the known and the unknown by intuiting a kind of esoteric 'Meta Narrative' that may very well constitute the basis of meaning itself. They place great value on the process of inner transformation and are constantly orienting themselves towards greater levels of depth through the integration of their own shadow material.

Due to their often solitary nature the Hermetics are somewhat harder to pinpoint within society, however they operate across many industries and cultural contexts often without ever revealing the true depth of their inner experience. They are found across various fields of research, are commonly drawn towards positions in academia and are the psychological depth workers amongst us. They also have an inclination towards any endeavour that involves the creation of new symbol sets and cultural narratives.

Effective Value Memes

And beyond these age related and vocation based demographics, a final common denominator amongst those likely to first join Collectives tends to be the system of 'cultural values' or 'value memes' they make use of to navigate through life. By 'value memes', I refer to a distinct spectrum of world views, belief structures and decision making frames that developmental psychologists have been mapping out since the mid 20th Century. In Beck and Cowans developmental model, known as Spiral Dynamics, the early adopters drawn to participate in Collectives would likely be described as having either a 'Green/Relativistic' or 'Yellow/Systemic' set of values, and in Hanzi Frienacht's model, such individuals would be typified as having either Postmodern or Metamodern values. For a deeper understanding of adult developmental psychology and the corresponding notion of effective value memes, I highly recommend reading Frienacht's book The Listening Society, in which he makes clear that any application of such models must be done with the utmost care, in order to ensure that such frameworks are used solely to create growth hierarchies which liberate us rather, than new dominator hierarchies which perpetuate the status quo.

So now that we have a clearer sense of what Collectives are, and the kinds of people likely to get involved, let's now take a look at how they can evolve and flourish over time.

15

Where It Can Take Us: Collective Dreams Of Tomorrow

Let's return now to our imagined Collective from Chapter 10, The Story Of Us. But this time we rejoin the group five years into the future, in the form of journal entry from one of the early members of the Collective, who is reflecting on all the ways the community has evolved.

1st June, 2025

'Our Collective has now fully matured and the size of the group has stabilised at around 120 people. Some of us participate in Collective activities most days of the week, while others are much less active, but still stay meaningfully engaged with the group by making sure they are present for key events. A number of children have been born to families in the collective and the parents feel lovingly supported by the huge array of extra 'aunties and uncles' that help out where ever they can. The young kids seem to benefit greatly from having so many different role models in their lives.

Some of us have moved into shared accomodation together and a couple of families have developed a co-housing arrangement where they live in separate houses on the same property, but share a kitchen, studio, laundry and garden space. There is talk amongst some members of buying a large piece of land in the countryside and establishing a residential community there, a place where we can grow our own food and spend time together outside of the hustle and bustle of the city.

Over the last couple of years, a number of us have collaborated on a series of successful social enterprises, including a thriving whole foods cafe and an event space that serves as a hub and meeting place for the entire community. Our monthly Open Mic has become a hugely popular event and extends an opportunity for those outside of our Collective to have a first hand experience of the loving and nurturing space we create when ever our community gathers together. We've raised money for a number of causes and funded the development of a community garden that is open to all members of the public.

One of the members in our Collective now sits on the local council and another is running for office in the upcoming state elections. An engineer in our group has been supported by the community in inventing a new way of producing renewable energy from compost, and a group of artists and musicians within the Collective have just collaborated on a performance piece that is designed to mobilise people towards becoming more effective activists for animal welfare.

But perhaps our greatest success has been the cultivation of such a strong sense of belonging and connection within the group. Over time, each of us has softened our more strident individual edges and begun to feel truly accepted and loved for who we are. We've become more vulnerable and real with each other and shared countless moments of great tenderness and joy. And as our bonds have deepened we take even more pleasure in witnessing each other blossom along the way.

There have challenging moments as well, and many of us have been openly confronted with coming to terms with our own limiting beliefs, patterns and insecurities. But ultimately, the group has been able to hold one another with loving compassion, and this has allowed each of us to lean into our shadows and continue integrating the parts of ourselves we've been doing our best to avoid. Whenever there has been conflict within the group, we've always taken the time to try and reconcile our differences, which has meant we've continuously improved upon our dispute resolution processes and gradually learned to become more graceful in our disagreements. Slowly but surely, as we come to terms with different kinds of trauma each of us are carrying around, we are learning how to express our anger and frustration in more healthy and productive ways.

A number of us have been held and supported through a variety of different crises in our lives. We've assisted each other in overcoming injuries, in coping with addiction and in recovering from trauma. We've taken the time to learn about each others lived experience of mental illness and disability. Some of us have received assistance in transitioning out of abusive relationships, others amongst us have been guided through the process of changing careers and been supported in finding new ways of generating income. And through all of this, we've continually encouraged one another to keep identifying and expressing our needs as they arise, which has enabled us to keep offering each other support, whilst also becoming more practiced at respecting and honouring our own boundaries in the process.

A few members from the group have started a second Collective in a city nearby, and the two communities have begun to cross pollinate each other. Both Collectives are now part of a vast and growing network of mutual aid communities that have begun to sprout up all over the world, and this broader movement is beginning to have a meaningful impact upon the fabric of wider society. We seem to be nearing ever closer to the tipping point where the sense of alienation so prevalent across modern society may finally be starting to give way to a joyous sense of regenerative reconnection. We're beginning to Collectively Bloom.'

* * *

This is just one of the many directions in which a mutual aid community can grow. In reality, each Collective will be wholly unique, as it will be co-created by a distinct group of people with a particular set of needs, values, aspirations and circumstances. And because each community will be a continuously evolving social ecosystem, constantly responding to changes in its surrounding environment, no two Collectives will develop in exactly the same way. Some will have a stronger focus on practices of authentic relating and psychological integration, others will be more geared towards activism or the launching of new kinds of social enterprise. And this points towards one of the more exciting aspects of the Collective Blooming narrative, the fact that each new community will be a wholly unique specimen, which means when they start to blossom, each one will produce a kind of communal flower that has never been seen before.

Personally, I hope to be a part of a Collective that combines together the best qualities of a number of different types of communities that have arisen throughout the ages. Such qualities include:

- The egalitarian ethic and connection to nature of a Palaeolithic tribe of Immediate Return Hunter Gatherers.
- The deeply peaceful collective resonance and humility of a third Century BCE Buddhist Sangha.
- The steady handed effectiveness and noble ethics of an 18th Century Quaker Social Enterprise.
- The artistic, philosophical and intellectual flair of a 1920's Parisian Salon.
- The optimism and good natured groundedness of a 1960's Back To The Land Commune.
- The emotional honesty, courage and compassion of one of Carl Rogers 1970's Encounter Groups.
- The (r)Evolutionary zeal of a modern day network of benevolent Anarcho-Hacktivists.

So now that we have a taste of what's possible, let's take a closer look at what it means to start finding our way back to community, and how such a journey can completely transform both our inner and outer worlds.

IV

The Path Of Transformation: Finding Our Way Back To Community

'We human beings have often been referred to as social animals. But we are not yet community creatures. We are impelled to relate with each other for our survival. But we do not yet relate with the inclusivity, realism, self-awareness, vulnerability, commitment, openness, freedom, equality, and love of genuine community. It is our task…to transform ourselves from mere social creatures into community creatures. It is the only way that human evolution will be able to proceed.' **M.Scott Peck**[31]

16

Tawai: Modernity's Missing Secret Sauce

For hundreds of thousands of years our species evolved to live in the wilderness, wandering the land with a close tribe of highly proficient humans around us at all times. In todays world, we find ourselves living out comparatively sedentary and isolated lifestyles, with the bulk of our time spent inside wholly artificial environments. If you add in a few thousand years of civilisation induced epigenetic trauma, as well as the inherent stress of trying to staying afloat in our fast paced capitalistic culture, then it's no wonder that so many of us struggle to feel truly at ease in the 21st Century.

And yet after being exposed to Indigenous wisdom a few pioneers from modern society appear to be actively rediscovering their inner sense of contentment by living in close communal kinship with people they hold dear. Bruce Parry is one such individual. After leaving the British Royal Marines to explore remote parts of the world, Bruce filmed an award winning documentary series called Tribe. Over a period of three years he lived with over fifteen different tribal societies, learning about their customs, experiencing their initiations and deeply immersing himself in their way of life. However, it wasn't until the very last episode of the series, when he

———

encountered the Penan people of Malaysia, that he seemed to have his worldview truly turned upside down.

As Bruce describes it, 'time spent with the Penan inspired me to realise that radically different ways of living together are not only possible, but might even be the best way for us to collectively flourish. Perhaps what we need is a new set of values, embedded in a different kind of story. An upgrade, perhaps, away from the belief that champions our individual pursuit of happiness and freedom as an inalienable right, toward one that sees us intrinsically linked to something larger than ourselves, and to which we should also feel a responsibility. Individual, but also a part of the whole.'[32]

In his search for what makes us human Bruce appears to have stumbled upon a kind of missing ingredient in our 21st Century way of life, what the Penan call Tawai. They describe it as an inner feeling of belonging that is like being held by the forest, a sense of deep and meaningful connection to one another and the natural world around them. And after experiencing a sense of Tawai himself, Bruce appears to have undergone a kind of metamorphosis and now acts as a kind of pathfinder for how we might be able to cultivate something akin to what the Penan experience, but in a modern day context.

Bruce's story symbolises the archetypal adventure of our modern age, a journey away from the precipice of alienation, and towards a state of being that will allow us to reconnect with each other and then collectively step into a whole new narrative together. His work shines a light on which ingredients are necessary for us to experience the kind enduring communal satisfaction that many tribal peoples still enjoy with one another. And like most secret sauces, the recipe is surprisingly simple:

1. **A Sense Of Connection** - Having regular interaction with a distinct group of people with whom we share the same values.
2. **A Sense Of Belonging** - Feeling seen, understood, accepted and celebrated for the many aspects that make us who we are.
3. **A Sense Of Contribution** - First identifying, and then offering up our unique gifts to our community, and feeling valued and appreciated for this.
4. **A Sense Of Purpose** - Feeling as if the interactions we share with our fellow community members are having a positive impact upon wider society.

Once you combine these elements together you begin the process of cultivating your very own human micro culture. So let's take a look now at what such life sized communal Petri dishes can empower us to achieve.

17

The Ultimate Petri Dish: Create Your Own Culture

One of the major benefits of forming Collectives is that it gives us an opportunity to co-create our very own micro cultures. After all, the cultures that most of us grew up in were largely dictated by our parents and our school administrators. And the workplace cultures we spend most of our adult lives within, are often exclusively shaped by the hyper competitive nature of our capitalistic system. This means that from cradle to grave we can find ourselves operating in cultural contexts that we've never really had a hand in shaping. Establishing communities of mutual aid invites us to buck this trend and actively participate in the cultivation of social ecosystems that are intended to empower, uplift and support each of the people within them.

This collective sense of cultural co-creation is similar in nature to what often occurs at music festivals around the world. Such events are all examples of liminal spaces where we're invited to step out of the norms of mainstream society, and for a brief moment, cultivate our very own cultural landscapes together. As B. Duffy writes 'at festivals we are culturally deprogrammed, allowing our hardened snake skins of certainty to be ceremoniously shed, leaving us pink and vulnerable, ready to face the immediate presence of true reality with eyes fully open.'[33] And participating in Collectives offers us a similar opportunity, the added bonus being that we get to continue nurturing such emergent cultural contexts in perpetuity. In this sense Collectives are like social Petri dishes that allow us to prototype new ways of living together, which if successful, over time, may also take root within wider society. As the systems theorist Buckminster Fuller famously declared 'you never change things by fighting the existing reality. To change something, build a new model that makes the existing model obsolete.'[34] And forming Collectives gives us an opportunity to do exactly that, to create small pockets of the kind of futures we wish to inhabit, right here in the world today. But rather than going it alone, or with just a couple of close friends, we get to run the experiment with up to two hundred other people who all share our same values and dreams.

This Petri dish effect also applies at an individual level. As when we join a Collective we're given the opportunity to gradually lower the masks we've been wearing and to begin to relate more authentically with ourselves and each other. And while this can be a challenging prospect at times, inviting us to confront our own biases, privileges and blind spots, we will be sharing the journey with a group of people all undergoing the same process, which means that we're perfectly positioned to support each other in more fully embodying our authentic selves along the way.

But perhaps the most important quality we can cultivate in such new cultural contexts, is that of safety.

———

As the trauma specialist Bessel Van Der Kolk surmises 'being able to feel safe with other people is probably the single most important aspect of mental health; safe connections are fundamental to meaningful and satisfying lives.'[35] Modern society is only just now beginning to come to terms with just how many of us have endured traumatic experiences during our upbringing and adult lives. This includes sexual abuse, various forms of discrimination and violence as well as the many forms of bullying that happen in our schools. The landmark Adverse Childhood Experiences study shed light on the fact that various forms of physical abuse and neglect are much more common than we previously thought. Which means that the cultivation of shared community spaces where people feel safe enough to let their guard down and start relaxing back into their bodies, may go a long way towards ensuring the future health of our societies.

When we fully embrace the vulnerability of being seen in community, it can be an incredibly transformational experience. Let's explore now what can unfold when we are courageous enough to welcome in the shared wisdom our Collective has to offer us.

18

Mirrored & Seen:
The Wisdom Of 100 Eyes

One of the many quirks of being human is that each one of us appears to come fully equipped with our very own psychological blind spots. We seem to need each other to help identify the self limiting patterns, habits and beliefs that we carry around with us. This is one of the reasons that joining a Collective can be so hugely beneficial to our personal growth and development, as it not only opens up the possibility of having our best qualities acknowledged and celebrated by the group, but also of having our shadow sides reflected back to us as well.

By tapping into the collective wisdom of the many trusted perspectives in our community, we gain the ability to form a kind of three hundred and sixty degree view of how we show up in the world. And if we're open to receive to it, such a multifaceted reflection of how we appear in the eyes of others can be a hugely beneficial tool in our journey towards greater levels of growth and integration. And while being so intimately seen can at times feel like a daunting prospect, in my experience it's almost always worth the risk, as when we have the courage to open up and reveal the more tender and vulnerable aspects of our ourselves, we create the opportunity to be loved and accepted for who we really are, which may be one of the most profoundly enriching human experiences we can have.

As Hanzi Freinacht puts it, 'it is often our highest hopes and dreams, the parts of ourselves that are most universal and most intimately held and cherished, that are not seen, heard, given recognition and successfully integrated into society. Hence, more and more people simply feel alienated. It is not really that the world has become a colder, lonelier place. It's just that the integration of these many unique souls is a more complicated and difficult matter. *Because* people have come farther in their (in)dividuation, more people also feel estranged, lonely and subtly dissatisfied.'[36] In other words when we begin to more fully blossom as individuals, we seem to require more complex and dynamic communal contexts to allow us to be held in our entirety. And this is precisely what Collectives are intended to do, to serve as crucibles of care for the most intimate and complex parts our inner selves to be lovingly acknowledged and appreciated by a group of people with whom we share respect and trust.

But when we increase the complexity of our communities, then we must also increase our ability to maintain healthy and supportive cultures within them. Part of this process involves learning to consider what kind of impacts the less integrated parts of our personalities may be having on the communities of people around us. After all, the large majority of us were raised in highly individualistic, overtly materialistic, systemically racist and wholly unsustainable cultures, so there is no shame in admitting that we may still have a long way to go in our personal journey of relearning how to engage with each other, and ourselves, from a place of sustained and compassionate understanding. But for this to happen, each of us may have to undergo a significant process of all encompassing transformation, a kind of metamorphosis from being mere Social Animals into that of truly Communal Creatures. Let's now take a closer look at what such a journey might look like.

19

Enter The Dojo:
Becoming A Community Creature

In order for us to collectively step into a new societal narrative, we'll first have to identify and evolve beyond the outdated narratives within ourselves. Plotting out a wider course for societal change is useful and essential, but it's infinitely more potent when it's matched with an ongoing process of individual transformation and personal behaviour change. As Dieter Duhm observes 'it is not possible to create a non-violent society when the impulses of hate and violence within are suppressed but not dissolved. A revolution that has not taken place inside cannot succeed outside. This is what we learn from history'.[37] And if we wish to undergo such an inner revolution, then joining a mutual aid community may be one of the best places to start, as the task of maintaining a baseline of functional harmony in such close knit social settings inevitably requires us to keep stepping up how we relate as individuals. Just as cultivating a practice of mediation can produce a certain set of results in our psyche, and being in a romantic partnership can compel us to master a specific kind of emotional maturity, it's been my experience that participating in true community can offer up it's own unique set of rewards.

—

For this reason I like to think of Collectives as the ultimate Dojos for the Self, a place where we can train to relate more compassionately and authentically with each other, and humbly turn to more experienced community members for guidance along the way. Such a process can be thought of as a journey towards becoming Community Creatures, a term I first came across in the work of M.Scott Peck. If I had to use just two words to describe the essential qualities of what I believe it means to be a Community Creature, they would be stable and fluid. A Community Creature is stable in the sense that they have a clear sense of what their strengths and weaknesses are, they know what they stand for and have developed an ability to identify and meet their own basic and complex needs. A Community Creature is fluid in that they are open to growth, not rigidly set in their ways, and dynamic enough to adapt their approach to harmonise with the ever evolving context of close knit community. From my experience with participating in community so far, these are two of the most important qualities that the 'Collective Dojo' gives us an opportunity to train in.

As Carl Jung was supposedly fond of saying, 'in sterquiliniis invenitur" or 'in filth it will be found'. Which alludes to the idea that what we most need to find will often be waiting where we least want to look. And when we participate in mutual aid communities we are provided with countless invitations to discover our very own diamonds in the muck. As undoubtedly, along the way, we will be faced with having to accommodate a broad range of differing opinions, to reach compromise on issues we feel passionately about and to move past conflicts that may have caused deep division within the group. And in moments such as these there is a very good chance that we'll be confronted with those aspects of ourselves that we might have been doing our best to avoid. It's also highly likely that at some point in our Collective journey we'll be invited to identify, and then ultimately let go of, many of the traces of hyperindividuality, rivalrous behaviour and dominator culture that we might have picked up from being raised within patriarchal and post-colonial societal models. And it's these exact kinds of experiences that while humbling when they arise, when embraced, can make participating in community such a deeply transformational experience.

But before we can become more graceful in our relations with others, we' often first have to cultivate a greater sense of harmony between the many aspects of our own self. In this sense it can be helpful to view ourselves as a kind of 'community of one', a sort of constantly shifting democracy of the many different sub personalities (or parts) that comprise our individual persona. There are a number of different psychological models that attempt to map out the many parts of our selves,[38] but one of the more comprehensive frameworks is that of Internal Family Systems (IFS) therapy, originally created by Richard C. Schwartz.

IFS provides a means for us to create a healthy sense of community within ourselves, by encouraging the different parts that make up who we are to dialogue with each other and develop a sense functional harmony. It's just one example of the kinds of modalities that can be 'trained with' in the Collective Dojo.[39] Some examples of other systems that can be collectively trained in include Non Violent Communication practices and Authentic Relating exercises. But naturally, over time, each Collective will settle upon its own set of preferred practices for empowering one another to relate more effectively with ourselves and each other.

As Richard Bartlett explores in his series of articles on Microsolidarity,[40] becoming a Community Creature involves finding harmony between the many aspects that compose our inner 'community of one', but also includes improving our ability to maintain highly cohesive relationships at the one to one level, 'Pod' level (3-6 people) and 'Collective' level (12-200 people). While experiencing greater levels of cohesion at each of these levels requires the mastery of different skills and abilities, the underlying process remains the same. It involves becoming actively aware of the kinds of subconscious patterns of behaviours which may be causing tension and misunderstanding in our relationships and then working towards increasing our capacity to respond more compassionately and skilfully to ourselves and others.

So far, my own experience in participating in community has shown me that I still have much psycho-emotional integration to do before I reach my own optimal levels of stable fluidity and that there are still many lessons for me to learn before I can consider myself a bonafide Community Creature. But I also recognise the huge amount of benefit I've received from being part of a community that has helped me to more fully know myself, and given me countless opportunities to be true to what I've discovered.

And as my self awareness has grown, I've become clearer on what it is I can offer up to the world, which seems be a common side effect of forming such deep connections with a group of people who fill us with inspiration. Let's take a closer look now at how participating in Collectives can help each of us get closer to our true calling in life. A process the Japanese refer to as finding our Ikigai.

20

Collective Incubation: Finding Your Ikigai

If it takes a village to raise a child, then it takes a community to forge a fully fledged adult. And this is largely due to the fact that whenever a committed group of open hearted individuals find themselves in true community, then they tend to actively assist each other in unearthing and developing their latent skills and abilities. At first this might be as simple as inspiring each other to try out a new instrument or to experiment with a particular form of meditation. But over time, it can be as profound as helping each other into a whole new vocation, or even assisting one another in discovering what the Japanese refer to as our Ikigai, which roughly translates into English as 'our reason for being'.

When we join a Collective we gain access to a community that can actively assist us in incubating new projects and skills. And this kind of ongoing support can often times be the deciding factor between whether we persevere with our endeavours or choose to throw in the towel. And such communal assistance can take many forms, it might manifest as one to one guidance, or as a request that everyone in our community leaves an online review for our new social enterprise. It can take the form of a working group that meets together each week with the explicit purpose of helping advance each others projects. It might entail buying a fellow community members new album or helping them to sell out their first ever fundraiser event for an important cause. It could even be as simple as recommending the right book at the right time or offering up a key introduction to someone in your wider network.

There are countless ways that being part of a Collective can empower us to move closer towards our dreams. But one of the more potent forms of support it makes available to us is the ability to request that others hold us accountable in following through on our stated goals and commitments. If we choose to embrace it, such accountability can be a hugely motivating and transformational force in our lives. As a long term community member once shared with the author M. Scott Peck 'we love each other too much to let anyone get away with anything'.[41] And this can most definitely include ensuring that those closest to us don't shy away from following through on what's most important to them.

But even as we come closer to discovering our reason for being, we still might find ourselves regularly weighed down by the immense amount of suffering and injustice we see in the world around us. We may become routinely overwhelmed by the fear that can arise when ever we stop to truly consider the epic scope of the many challenges facing our species. So let's take a look now at how joining a Collective might help us to more effectively face up to, and come to terms with, the psychological burdens of living through such turbulent and uncertain times.

21

Atlas Squared: Easing The Weight Of The World

Our brains were wired to consider the wellbeing of around one hundred and fifty other people.[42] But our modern communications technology now connects us to the daily plight of billions of other sentient beings. Many of these people (and animals) are already enduring lives of extreme hardship, and with the looming prospect of climate breakdown on our very near horizon, their situations are likely to get a lot worse before they get any better.

Participating in Collectives provides us with an opportunity to meaningfully engage with the issues of our time without leaving us feeling burnt out, overwhelmed or alone. By staying in close contact with an equally committed group of change makers we can share the triumphs and tribulations we experience in ongoing our efforts to effect change, and support each other along the way. After all, our species has a long history of coping with turbulent times and terrifying threats, the only difference these days is that it largely feels as if we are facing the challenges on our own, devoid of the loving support of a competent tribe. But by participating in mutual aid communities we can rediscover this sense of being in it together, as when we walk side by side, working together towards a common

---

cause, what once seemed impossible can all at once begin to seem possible, or even probable.

When we mourn the extreme levels of suffering in the world together as a community, we can be held and hold others as we each go through our own personal cycles of grief, or what the Germans refer to as Weltschmerz (a deep sadness about the imperfection of the world). Such communal solidarity can get us through our darkest moments and ensure we rediscover our resolution and capacity to act. As no matter how big a particular threat may appear to be, everything feels so much more manageable when ever we have a close group of proficient humans surrounding us. As the old saying goes, a problem shared is a problem halved, and with the prospect of total ecological collapse on our radar, we're more desperately in need of such communal support than ever before. Let's take a closer look now at just how valuable such support networks can be during times of societal unrest.

22

Trust Networks: The One True Currency

The COVID-19 pandemic has revealed that even our highly technical societies are still acutely vulnerable to crisis. It's showed us that our governments are often ill equipped to deal with the kinds of borderless challenges (pandemics, mass migration, food shortages, increasing natural disasters) that will continue to arise in the decades to come and highlighted just how over dependent we've become on a relatively fragile network of global supply chains. The pandemic has impacted everyone and dispelled the illusion that any of us can remain wholly insulated from the underlying issues that now threaten the stability of our socio-economic systems. For better or worse, it's reminded us that we're all in this together.

Before the pandemic, the idea that at some point in the near future we may need to depend upon our local community to see us through a time of crisis may have seemed alarmist. But after experiencing what it's like to have our supermarket shelves laid bare, it's now much easier to appreciate just how important it is that we begin decentralising various aspects of our economies and foster a vast network of empowered local communities. We can no longer ignore the fact that we're almost all entirely dependent upon a system that at any point is just a few days away from grinding to a halt. If the power cuts out the supermarket trucks don't deliver, or if oil

81

production stops within a matter of hours many of us are left helpless and exposed. After our collective experience of COVID-19, it's now clearer than ever that the highly atomised nature of modern society leaves us acutely vulnerable to a wide range of existential threats.

Forming mutual aid communities can not only bring joy, inspiration, growth and belonging into our lives, it also just happens to be one of the best ways to ensure we can both survive and thrive during times of hardship. After all, there's nothing more empowering than being a part of an adaptable and resilient support network that can respond quickly in times of emergency and has enough people and skills within it to ensure that all of its members are safe and cared for during times of need. Numerous studies into how we respond to disaster situations have shown that social support is the most powerful protection we have against becoming overwhelmed by stress and trauma.[43] Collectives can offer us this kind of social safety net and provide us with a space to return to where we feel safe, loved and supported. This may be the most valuable currency of all.

In Conclusion:
Let The Experiment Begin

'When asked if I am pessimistic or optimistic about the future, my answer is always the same: If you look at the science about what is happening on earth and aren't pessimistic, you don't understand data. But if you meet the people who are working to restore this earth and the lives of the poor, and you aren't optimistic, you haven't got the pulse.' **Paul Hawken**[44]

* * *

At some point in our headlong rush towards 'progress', we cut ourselves off from the communal crucible of close human connection that nurtured our species for hundreds of thousands of years. Since we first settled into agricultural civilisation we've engineered a series of socio-economic systems that have incentivised us to consistently exploit one another and degrade our supporting ecosystems, right up until the point that they inevitably collapse. And now, as we continue to undermine the health of our forests, fisheries, aquifers, arable land and atmosphere, we edge ever closer to the biggest collapse of all, that of our 21st Century globalised economy.

Caught in whirlwinds of consumption, we've unwittingly substituted the sacred for the profane, prioritised convenience over compassion and, in the process, begun to lose touch with our ability to live together as conscious, caring and cooperative creatures of community.

And yet despite the calamitous trajectory we find ourselves on, we remain a highly adaptable species that is capable of creating and sharing inspiring new narratives that can allow us to quickly pivot in whole new directions. But the stories we've been culturally indoctrinating ourselves with are in urgent need of upgrading. After decades of Neoliberalism we've seen a resurgence of Nationalist Populism, a narrative which appears woefully incapable of fostering the kind of global cooperation that is required to deal with the existential threats we now face. But the even deeper story we'll have to identify and uproot is that of Hollow & Oppressive Economic Materialism, a belief system with a myopic focus on never ending growth that more often than not leaves us with an inner sense of numbness as it continuously compels us to scramble for ever more status and wealth.

The good news is that there are already many alternative and regenerative narratives ready for us to pick up and embrace. Each of these new societal stories imagines a time when we join together to recreate a more compassionate and peaceful world. They frame the looming catastrophes on our doorstep as a collective call to adventure, an invitation to rediscover one another and in the process cultivate whole new ways of being. A Collective Blooming is one such narrative, it's an invitation to envision a planet wide network of peaceful, decentralised, ecologically sustainable and socially just communities. An invitation to start working towards the realisation of a Compassionate Global Village, where the health of all living beings inner worlds, relationships and communal bonds are placed at the centre of our political and economic agendas.

To realise such a world we'll have to experiment with whole new ways of relating with each other and then leverage the resulting synergy towards creating a global movement of change. One of the natural places to start this journey is at the community level, where we have a direct opportunity to come together and begin prototyping more sustainable, compassionate and joyful ways of living together. Through prototyping new forms of mutual aid community such as the Conscious Change Collective, we'll have the opportunity to foster our own thriving micro cultures of human interaction, and embed ourselves in the kind of reciprocal trust networks that can radically increase our ability to cope with any societal crises that may emerge. We'll be invited to continually keep levelling up as individuals and be actively encouraged to use our skills and abilities to help bring about positive change in the world. We'll be supported in shouldering the psychological burden of reshaping our societal structures as we collectively rediscover the inherent joy of becoming Community Creatures.

This journey back into a shared sense of communal belonging will likely prove challenging at times. We'll have to risk exposing our tender hearts to those around us and may have to let go of many of our limiting beliefs and behaviours along the way. But as we careen towards ecological collapse, it seems we have little choice other than to come together and push for sweeping change.

—

And beyond the reward of securing the health of our biosphere for generations to come, we may just rediscover a kind of deep communal satisfaction that most of us in the modern world had forgotten was even possible.

A felt sense of connection, belonging and togetherness that so invigorates the human condition that we're left smiling at days end, eager for the challenges ahead and grateful for the system wide transformation they will bring. It's time for us to rediscover each other, it's time to Collectively Bloom.

Appendix I. The Finer Details: The FAQ's Of Getting Collective

Included below is a list of frequently asked questions in relation to forming and participating in Collectives. But first, a caveat. Because the particular preferences and needs of every mutual aid community will be wholly unique, there is no one 'right way' to set up and run a Collective. Which means that the slightly unsatisfying answer to many of questions below tends to be, 'it depends on the needs of the group'. The whole idea after all is to come together in community and decide for ourselves how best to support and empower each other. However, with this in mind, I thought it still might be useful to share my own attempts at answering some of the key questions that tend to be raised when people are first introduced to the idea of forming or joining a Conscious Change Collective.

1. How did you get involved with this? Are you part of a Collective?
2. What are the major purposes of forming a Collective?
3. What are some of the benefits of joining a Collective?
4. How do Collectives get started?
5. How many people are there in each Collective?
6. What kind of things do people in a Collective do together?

7. How are decisions made and how is power distributed within a Collective?

8. What are Pods and why are they so central to the Collective experience?

9. Does everyone in a Collective live together or at least near each other? Can a Collective be solely online?

10. Are people in a Collective expected to share their money or finances together? Do people earn income together?

11. How do people in the collective communicate with each other?

12. Where do Collective meetings and activities take place?

13. Does there need to be a clear boundary between who is in or out of a Collective? Is there a specific membership model?

14. Roughly how often do people in a Collective meet up or interact with each other?

15. How do people get selected or invited to join a collective?

16. How can we ensure that forming Collectives doesn't simply lead to more division and separation in the world?

17. How can we encourage diversity and ensure people of every age, race, gender, economic status and sexual preference (etc.) feel invited into, and included within, each Collective?

18. How do Collectives relate to stepping into a new societal narrative together? Can they really create wider systemic change?

19. Are there any Collectives out there already that I can learn about or join?

20. What type of values, intentions and guidelines might a Collective choose to adopt?

21. Isn't this how cults start? How can we avoid such unhealthy dynamics forming within a Collective?

22. What are some of the major challenges and pitfalls of forming and participating in Collectives?

23. Can forming Collectives really help us address our most pressing societal issues & existential challenges as a species?

24. Are Collectives better suited to rural or urban environments?

25. How do Collectives relate to the concept of Metamodernism?

26. How can we help to minimise any sense of exclusion that might arise in those people that haven't been invited to join a particular Collective or Pod?

27. How do we deal with the fact that joining such close knit communities can often compel us to subtly conform to the cultural median of the group?

28. How can Collectives learn from the wisdom of the worlds Indigenous people and foster a meaningful connection to the land?

29. How are Collectives different from a close friendship group, a Mens or Womens group, or any other kind of growth focused or change making community?

30. How can Collectives ensure that they take into account the needs of people living with disabilities and various types of health conditions?

31. Is everyone in the Collective expected to have similar political, dietary or religious/spiritual preferences?

32. Is it possible to be part of more than one collective at a time?

33. What are some examples of the kinds of working groups that might form within a Collective?

34. Is there a particular methodology for resolving conflicts within a Collective?

35. What happens if someone in a Collective continually violates the rules or guidelines of the group?

36. How might Collectives help to counteract the racism that is endemic to modern society?

37. Is there a minimum level of engagement required to stay a part of a Collective?

38. How can Collectives cater to the needs and desires of Introverts & Highly Sensitive People?

39. Will there be whole families in each Collective? Should I invite my Mum along too?

40. What role will ritual play in the Collective experience?

1. How did you get involved with this? Are you part of a Collective?

My journey with forming Collectives began with a desire to design and build Ecovillages. But after becoming involved with a community cafe and events space I soon realised that it was possible to cultivate a strong sense of belonging and support between a group of people without having to live together on the same piece of land. A few of us proposed to our wider community that we might like to experiment with forming a rudimentary kind of Proto-Collective. That was in late 2016, and since then around 150 of us have been deepening our shared story ever since.

2. What are the major purposes of forming a Collective?

- To act as a container for an experience of transformational community.
- To help us to grow, evolve and become more integrated individuals.
- To act as a catalyst for responding to the challenges we face as a species.
- To create new ways and opportunities for us to express ourselves and have fun together.
- To empower ourselves and each other to do more meaningful work with our lives.
- To act as petri dishes for the creation of a new kind of regenerative culture.

3. What are some of the benefits of joining a Collective?

- To experience an increased sense of community, belonging and connection.

- To be able to give and receive support from a group of people you care about and who care about you.

- To learn more about your self and grow as a person.

- To provide an opportunity to actively engaged with making a difference in the world.

4. How do Collectives get started?

So far I've identified two major approaches for starting a new Collective. The first approach involves inviting members of a pre-existing community to officially form a Collective. The second approach involves starting from scratch, which is likely to begin with the formation of a Pod (containing between 3-6 people), and then grow from there as those first Pod members gradually invite other people to join.

In his article 'How to Weave Social Fabric' Richard Bartlett outlines his own specific approach for forming mutual aid communities. It begins with an individual or small group of initiators calling in a group of people to a Gathering (usually a multiday residential event) in order to share in a series of peak bonding experiences together. He then suggests making use of the momentum and sense of cohesion that a Gathering can create in order to form a series of Crews (his term for Pods). This then forms the context for people to begin practicing what Richard has dubbed Microsolidarity, which he describes as 'a kind of personal development, in good company, for social benefit.'[46]

5. How many people are there in each Collective?

I would suggest the minimum number of people for a group to be considered a Collective is anything over the size of a single Pod (ie. larger than 6 people). And I would put the the maximum number somewhere around 250 people, as this is the upper range of Dunbars number, a cognitive limit to the amount of people with which anthropological research suggests we can maintain familiar and stable social relationships.

6. What kind of things do people in a Collective do together?

This will vary widely depending on the interests and values of the particular Collective. See Chapter 11 for a list of examples.

7. How are decisions made and power distributed within a Collective?

Each Collective will decide for itself how best to allocate power and responsibility, as well how to make decisions as a group. Though broadly I would say the balance to aim for is between giving everyone in the Collective as much of a sense of agency and involvement in the decision making process as possible, whilst also ensuring that the process is not so time consuming or complicated that people stop engaging. Here is a list of some of example structures for making decisions and allocating power:

The Working Groups Model

- Specific working groups are formed around the different functions within the community. Each working group then makes decisions related to their own domain of responsibility on behalf of the rest of the Collective. One member of each working group is then chosen to participate in a meta group that helps to oversee the entire Collective.

- Sociocracy is one version of this model that emphasises consent (we don't strongly disagree) over consensus (we all completely agree) and includes a number of other specific practices for how to operate each working group, which in the Sociocratic lingo are known as a Circles.

The Elected Council Model

- A small group of people are selected (or voted in) by the Collective to act as decision makers for a certain period of time.

The Direct Democracy Model

- All decisions that are deemed important by the Collective are determined by a vote. Generally each member is given one vote.

- Due to recent advancements in blockchain and token technology there are a number of emerging alternatives to the Direct Democratic model. These include Liquid Democracy (which allows people to vest their voting power with various delegates) and Quadratic Voting (which allows people to express the degree of their preferences rather than just the direction of their preferences).

The Sole Representative Model

- One person acts as the final decision maker for the entire Collective for a distinct period of time. They may form a team to support them or choose to oversee the formation of a series of working groups.
- They are either selected or voted in by the whole Collective, or else they are chosen, overseen and supported by a Board, which is also either selected by or voted in by the whole Collective.

The Anarchic Model

- There are no chosen representatives and people participate as they wish based on their particular preferences at the time.
- There may be an agreed upon process for the majority of Collective members voting to be able to request changes or put a stop to a particular project, or the activities of a certain member, if they are deemed to be doing more harm than good.

- Peoples actions may, or may not be supported by a set of guidelines or a kind of constitution.

This is just a small list of potential models, there are many more variations that Collectives can choose to make use of in governing themselves.

8. What are Pods and why are they so central to the Collective experience?

Pods are where a lot of the deepest experiences of belonging, support and growth tend to occur. They are groups of between 3-6 people that form within a Collective in order to share in a particular type of experience.

They can be conducted in person or online and depending upon the needs and wishes of the particular Pod, they can happen over a period of weeks, months or even go on indefinitely. Here is a list of examples:

- **Circling Pods** - A form of peer to peer group therapy where participants come together to share about their inner experiences and receive support around any challenges they might be facing in their lives.

- **Learning Pods** - A group of people that come together to study a certain course, subject or approach to personal development.

- **Enterprise & Project Pods** - A group of people that either directly undertake a new project or social enterprise together, or else support each other in further developing projects or businesses they already run.

- **Goals & Accountability Pod** - A group of people that come together to set goals and then support each other to stay accountable in moving towards them.
- **Skill Share Pods** - A group of people that take turns in teaching each other particular skills or expertise.
- **Activism Pods** - A group of people that work together to progress a particular cause.

There are countless different ways that Pods of people can come together to support and empower each other, and the high level of intimacy, trust and depth they allow for is one of the most transformational aspects of the whole Collective experience.

9. Does everyone in a Collective live together or at least near each other? Can a Collective be solely online?

People can live where ever they choose and still participate in a Collective. However living close enough to be able to regularly participate in activities and events together will naturally allow for a much more intimate and cohesive community experience. Some Collectives may choose to allow members to participate remotely, others may be conducted largely online and perhaps only encourage members to gather in person once or twice a year, if at all.

10. Are people in a Collective expected to pool their money or finances? Do people earn income together?

There is no expectation for anyone to share their finances with other people in their Collective. Some Collectives will be run without a budget, relying wholly on voluntary contributions. Others may collect a fee from members or else be funded from the proceeds of a Collective enterprise. Another possibility is to set up a kind of expanded Tool Library and share the use of certain possessions (such as tools, bikes, cars, instruments, sporting equipment etc).

Over time, certain members of each community will likely begin collaborating with each other on projects that earn income, and may then decide to allocate a portion of this revenue towards covering any costs of running the Collective.

Such a Collective fund can also be utilised for seeding new projects and enterprises within the community. Some freelancers within the Collective may also choose to experiment with pooling together a percentage of their revenue and then distributing it amongst themselves.

* * *

11. How do people in the collective communicate with each other?

There are a number of different online tools that people in a Collective can use to communicate. They include:

- Instant Messaging Groups
- Social Media Groups
- Online Group Decision Making Tools
- Online Group Project Management Tools

However, wherever possible, a healthy balance of online and in person communication is encouraged, as more regular face to face interactions tend to weave much stronger community bonds.

12. Where do Collective meetings and activities take place?

Collective meetups, meetings and activities can happen anywhere. Depending on the type of activity they might be held in peoples homes, in a shared work space or in a local cafe. It's definitely beneficial to have a space (or a number of them) that members of a Collective feel to be a kind of home base. This might take the form of a particular cafe or co-working space managed by the Collective, or perhaps by one of its members. However having such a definitive home base is by no means a prerequisite for forming a Collective, as much of the community experience happens in small groups or Pods that can be held in a wide variety of spaces.

13. Does there need to be a clear boundary between who is in or out of a Collective? Is there a specific membership model?

To cultivate a deep sense of belonging and trust I believe it's essential to establish clear boundaries between whether someone is or isn't a member of a Collective. It will be up to each Collective to decide whether they will have one level of membership or various tiers of involvement and responsibility.

14. Roughly how often do people in a Collective meet up or interact with each other?

This will vary widely depending upon the culture of each particular Collective, and the personal preferences of each of the individuals within it. However, if one of the aims is to share the flow of life together, then having regular opportunities to interact is essential. I would say a minimum level of interaction to remain engaged and connected to the culture of a Collective would involve attending at least one event or activity per month.

Over the last few years, on average I have personally participated in around 3-4 community based activities each week. However, this doesn't include the various one to one meet ups with friends in my community, or meetings for projects I'm undertaking with other community members. My engagement level has been towards the higher end within my community, with many others choosing to only engage around once a week.

15. How do people get selected or invited to join a collective?

Each Collective will evolve its own approach to inviting new people in. Some may have a working group that is responsible for the task, other's may have a system where every current member of the Collective has to approve of any new invitees before they are accepted into the group. No matter the approach, it's useful to have a number of mechanisms for potential members to get to know others in the Collective before officially being welcomed in. This may include inviting people to participate in Collective Gatherings, Open Mics, gardening days or Skill Share workshops.

16. How can we ensure that forming Collectives doesn't simply lead to more division and separation in the world?

The 'us and them' trap that humans have been falling into for thousands of years is one of the greatest risks of forming such communal groups. As when a Collective comes together there is always a potential that its members will begin to see themselves as separate from, or somehow more superior than the rest of society. As history has shown us this kind of thinking can result in some very violent outcomes. As such whenever a Collective is started it's wise to repeatedly highlight the intention of coming together in order to be of benefit to all living beings and then to cultivate a sense of group culture around this particular intention. Along the way this can be re-enforced by ensuring that each Collective offers up value outside of itself and provides a number of benefits to the wider community in which it's embedded. Being as transparent as possible around how the Collective is run is another way to minimise any sense of separation from people outside of the group.

It's also important to be aware of any 'High School' dynamics that may emerge within a Collective. This is where an inner group of friends, whether they mean to or not, begin to engender an overt sense of exclusivity. While it is natural that small groups of friends will wish to spend time together, the Collective will benefit greatly from its participants expanding the traditional concept of 'coolness' to include as many people as possible and for it's members to always practice seeing each other not as stereotypes, but rather as totally unique bundle of experiences, characteristics and gifts.

17. How can we encourage diversity and ensure people of every age, race, gender, economic status and sexual preference feel invited into, and included within each Collective?

While each Collective will craft its own approach for ensuring a healthy level of diversity within the group, I personally believe that as long as everyone is in alignment with the core values of the Collective, then it's preferable to go for as much diversity as possible. I feel that practicing the successful honouring and integration of a wide range of world views, beliefs and cosmologies within one community container is one of the more profound opportunities that forming Collectives can provide us with.

However, for a number of reasons people from similar demographics with similar interests tend to congregate together in groups. So if a broad level of diversity is truly desired by a Collective, then its members will have to actively work towards reaching out to a wide range of potential participants, including the historically marginalised members of society. Maintaining such diversity within a Collective also requires the cultivation of a culture where there is welcome space for all of the different voices to be heard, considered and celebrated within the community. The creation of such a culture may necessitate a series of uncomfortable conversations around systemic oppression and privilege, which may bring to light a number of biases and prejudices members of the Collective may not have even realised they were harbouring.

18. How do Collectives relate to stepping into a new societal narrative together? Can they really create wider systemic change?

Collectives can encourage us to adopt new societal narratives by acting as cultural Petri dishes where we can cultivate and experiment with new ways of living together. They are places where new stories can emerge, take root, blossom and then go to seed, hopefully spreading far and wide across different parts of society. They bring about systemic change by:

- Nurturing members with a sense of belonging and support, thus empowering them to become even more effective in the kinds of activism and changing making projects in which they already involved.
- Acting as the catalyst for new world changing projects to be launched by members of the group.
- Serving as a space to prototype and beta test new ways of living together and organising our selves.

19. Are there any Collectives out there already that I can learn about or join?

The closest thing to a fully fledged Collective that I've come across (that has a public profile) is the Enspiral network based in Wellington, New Zealand. They have made their handbook publicly available online, and some of their members have also published a book called Better Work Together which details many of the lessons they have learned in their quest to help each other do more meaningful work. Other examples of 'Collective like communities' include:

- The New Republic Of The Heart Practice Community.
- The concept of the Proto-B as described by Jim Rutt.
- The community of residents at the Monastic Academy.

There must be many more examples out there that go by other names, and I'm looking forward to encountering more of them in the years to come.

20. What type of values, intentions and guidelines might a Collective choose to adopt?

While each Collective will co-create its own set of values, intentions and guidelines, here is a list of examples:

- **Building Community** - Building & weaving a resilient sense of community where everyone feels connected and part of something bigger.
- **Celebrating Creativity** - Celebrating each others creativity through making and sharing our art and music.
- **Fostering Cohesion** - Fostering deep and meaningful interaction between people from different age groups, races, genders, nations & walks of life.
- **Advancing Social Justice & Equity** - Working to create a more just and equitable world. Focusing on both local and global causes.
- **Forming Friendships** - Forming vibrant relationships with each other.
- **Seeking Growth & Transformation** - Inspiring and supporting one another along a path of transformational growth.
- **Creating Healing & Integration** - Nurturing and healing our minds and bodies.
- **Honouring Ecology** - Rebalancing our relationship with nature and ensuring the health of our surrounding ecosystems.

- **Cultivating Awareness** - Taking the journey inward towards becoming more conscious and mindful human beings.

- **Inter-Community Connection** - Connecting up and collaborating with other communities in our region and around the world.

- **Providing Support & Guidance** - Acting as a support network to assist each other in overcoming any challenges we may be facing.

- **Growing Social Enterprise** - Helping one another launch and grow sustainable and ethical enterprises that make a difference in the world.

21. Isn't this how cults start? How can we avoid such unhealthy dynamics forming within a Collective?

It can be, which is why whenever we start or join a Collective we should be well aware of common cult dynamics and how to avoid them. Here are some signs to be watchful for:

- There is a highly charismatic leader who demands total loyalty from the group and seeks to be worshipped.
- Members are strongly encouraged not to leave and are penalised when they do.
- There is complete authoritarianism without any accountability.
- Questioning, doubt and dissent are discouraged or even punished.

- The use of mind altering experiences to suppress doubts about the group and its leader.

Ensuring there is transparency in how things operate, a healthy diversity in thought and accountability mechanisms for anybody in a position of authority are all ways to counterbalance any cult like dynamics that can begin to form within a community. For more information I recommend the book Cults Inside Out by Rick Allen Ross.

22. What are some of the major challenges and pitfalls of forming and participating in Collectives?

'All happy families are alike; each unhappy family is unhappy in its own way.' Leo Tolstoy began his novel Anna Karenina with that observation and Collectives are no different. While they can bring untold levels of joy and growth into our lives, there are countless ways in which they can become overwhelming, turbulent and fractious. Here is just a short list of some of the major challenges and pitfalls I've encountered so far:

Time Pressure - Many peoples lives already feel overly full with just the commitments they already have to their family, friends and workplaces. So despite all the benefits of joining a Collective, adding in another layer of responsibility and engagement can sometimes feel overwhelming.

The Potential Solution - Create a check in mechanism to ensure that people are not becoming overburdened by Collective responsibilities and that no one feels pressured to engage beyond what for them is a sustainable level of interaction.

Political & Moral Disagreements - Debates around political, social and economic issues can lead to deep schisms within a group. As people unearth various aspects of their individual and collective shadow, conflicts can arise around how best to approach and integrate these parts of ourselves. Differing views around how best to enact wider system change can also lead to tension.

The Potential Solution - Early on work to create a culture of healthy dialogue and debate around difficult issues within the Collective and take the time to establish supportive environments for everyone's voice to be heard and respectfully considered.

Loss Of Privacy - Being part of a Collective can create a kind of 'small town effect' where a large group of people come to know a lot about what is going on in each others lives. In essence this can mean we trade some of our anonymity and potentially some of our privacy in order to establish a close sense of communal connection with others. And if the right structures, boundaries and protocols are not put into place from the beginning, this can sometimes lead to scenarios where we are left feeling over exposed.

The Potential Solution - Ensuring that everyone actively commits to safeguarding and respecting each others privacy and confidentially every step of the way. Creating a policy around which aspects of the Collective experience are to be kept private is also a helpful strategy. As is periodically discussing the Collectives approach to maintaining privacy and regularly checking in as a group as to how everyone is feeling in regards to the issue.

Burnout - A small group of people can often find themselves doing the lions share of the work in regards to keeping a Collective running and ensuring there is a healthy culture within the group. This can often go on behind the scenes and before long these individuals may soon find themselves feeling exhausted and overburdened.

The Potential Solution - Keep enquiring as to whether there are one or two individuals carrying too much Collective weight and find ways to support them.

Changing Relationships - Being in a Collective context with close friends can sometimes significantly change the nature of those relationships. While working together towards increasing levels of personal growth, and collaborating with one another on world changing projects often leads to an even stronger kind of bond, it can also take away some of the light heartedness and ease of simply being friends. Similar in a way to when we start working in the same business as a romantic partner, it can change things, some times for the better and sometimes for the worse, and it's good to be aware of this fact before joining a Collective.

The Potential Solution - Be conscious of how working together on projects can change the nature of important relationships and perhaps allocate some extra time for simply having fun with those close friends who are also in our Collective.

Patience Tested - To experience the joy and belonging of close knit community we also need to accept that sometimes certain individuals are just going to leave us feeling frustrated and annoyed. Hopefully we can be successful in creating a culture where such experiences can be leaned into and used to further our levels of self awareness and growth. However even with these mechanisms in place, we still need to be ready to take the good with the bad and accept that sometimes we are just going be left feel frustrated, disappointed and annoyed by the people we are close to.

The Potential Solution - Ensure there are mechanisms for everyone in the Collective to be able to share their grievances and frustrations with some one close to them, perhaps even creating some kind of buddy system that ensures everyone has access to a receptive and supportive ear within the group.

* * *

23. Can forming Collectives really help us address our most pressing societal issues & existential challenges as a species?

While cultivating community might not seem like the most direct way to avoid catastrophic climate change or reduce the chances of nuclear war, I believe that the kinds of interpersonal skills we receive from participating in Collectives can significantly increase our capacity to create change in the world.

Collectives can also provide us with the inspiration, support and accountability to meaningfully engage with the most pressing social issues of the day. When we are part of a group that actively educates itself around human rights abuses, racial injustice, animal rights, biodiversity loss and oppression of minority groups (just to name a few), we are much more likely to be able to start taking the kinds of actions that will help to make a difference. And being part of a community that regularly discusses and engages with these issues can help to ensure we don't feel alone in the face of such complex and multifaceted issues.

Collectives can also help to increase our capacity as individual agents of change. By offering us a place to process any difficulties, resistances and blockages we may be experiencing in our lives, mutual aid communities can serve to increase our sense of resilience and ensure that we stay inspired and supported enough to keep making a difference however we can. And over time as a global network of fully formed Collectives begins to emerge, the direct impact of all the projects they will undertake may prove to be a significant factor in our transition towards a truly regenerative societal narrative.

24. Are Collectives better suited to rural or urban environments?

Collectives can flourish in either context as long as there is enough people in one area that share similar values and a commitment to cultivating community together. If there are only a small number of people in any particular region that fit this criteria, then forming a pod is another way to start experiencing a deep sense of solidarity with others. It's also possible to participate online in a Collective from a wholly remote location, so this is another option for people as well.

25. How do Collectives relate to the concept of Metamodernism?

The Metamoderna website defines Metamodernism as a 'philosophy and view of life that corresponds to the digitalized, postindustrial, global age. This can be contrasted against modern and postmodern philosophies.' And as the author Hanzi Frienacht describes 'the metamodern view is to support the necessary reintegration of highly dividuated modern people into deeper community—or Gemeinschaft—but to do so with great sensitivity towards the inescapable risks of new, subtler forms of oppression.'[46] And he continues 'I believe that we would—we must—plunge head-on into the mysteries of existence, not as individuals, but as an evolving global network of posthuman transindividuals, living in volitionally organized virtual tribes.'[47] Forming Collectives dove tails very closely with such a Metamodern vision of the future.

26. How can we help to minimise any sense of exclusion that might arise in those people that haven't been invited to join a particular Collective or Pod?

Whenever a group forms that has a clear distinction between who is a member and who isn't, there is a good chance that some people on the peripheries may feel either excluded or left out. However such a dynamic can be pre-empted, and any Pods or Collectives that form can function in a way to minimise the likelihood of such feelings of exclusion arising within the wider community within which they exist. This can be achieved by:

- Being clear and transparent about the groups policies of inclusion and exclusion.
- Offering information and guidance to others around how to form their own Pods or Collectives if such groups that already exist are at full capacity.
- Offering individuals a potential pathway to later inclusion (through self study or mentorship) if for what ever reason they don't currently align with the criteria or values of the group but still wish to join.

* * *

27. How do we deal with the fact that joining close knit communities can often compel us to subtly conform to the cultural median of the group?

Monkey see, monkey do. Just like our primate cousins, when ever we join a new community, we can often find ourselves being subtly pulled towards the cultural median of the group. This can lead us to change our dietary habits, influence the way we dress and shift our political views, often without us realising that it's even happening. And depending on community in question, this can either be a positive or negative dynamic for the individuals within it, but in either case I believe it's important to take steps towards ensuring everyone remains as conscious as possible of the subtle tides of influence that operate within each and every Collective.

This might involve holding regular community discussions that are designed to identify and describe the various cultural currents at play within the group. It might also entail facilitating sharing circles around the questions of conformity and what behaviours and actions tend to either increase or decrease peoples status within the community. Ideally, over time, we could even begin to consciously select which kind of actions and behaviours we would like to be celebrated and modelled by the group, essentially then utilising our tendency towards accumulating status to hasten our growth and development.

* * *

28. How can Collectives learn from the wisdom of the worlds Indigenous people and foster a meaningful connection to the land?

Many Indigenous peoples have lived in harmony with their surrounding ecologies for hundreds of thousands of years. These cultures not only have extensive knowledge around how to live sustainably in close knit community structures, but they are also much more intimately connected to the land, and if they are willing to share their wisdom, there is much to be learned. So if a Collective is established in a region where there are still people with Indigenous wisdom, then it is highly recommended to respectfully try and establish a dialogue and relationship with these members of the community. In my opinion any kind of truly regenerative community will have a strong and sensitive connection to the land on which it lives. Having any understanding of the traditional story of that land is a critical component of this.

29. How are Collectives different from a close friendship group, a Mens or Womens group, or any other kind of growth focused or change making community that already exists?

Collectives share many similar qualities with friendship groups and other kinds of community structures. However what makes Collectives broadly unique is the primary intention of cultivating a deep sense of belonging and community together along side a focus on bringing about positive change in wider society. More specifically, this manifests as a focus on the the seven different types of practices outlined in Chapter 11. These practices include:

- Waking Up
- Tuning In
- Leaning In
- Integrating In
- Levelling Up
- Throwing Down
- Giving Back

30. How can Collectives ensure that they take into account the needs of people living with disabilities and various types of health conditions?

It is critical that people living with disabilities, chronic illness and mental health conditions all feel welcomed and able to meaningfully participate in Collectives. This requires the cultivation of a specific culture of awareness and sensitivity around each persons individual needs, whilst also making sure that no one is stigmatised for their disabilities or physical condition. An important part of this process is to create opportunities to carefully listen and learn about each others lived experience of day to day life, as such a shared sense of understanding not only ensures everyone feels better understood, but can also ensure that creative solutions are found which allow everyone to participate in Collective activities in their own unique way.

31. Is everyone in a Collective expected to have similar political, dietary or religious/spiritual preferences?

Ensuring that everyone in a Collective shares the same values will often also result in a broad alignment of lifestyle choices and personal beliefs. However, each Collective will have to decide for itself how tolerant they wish to be in terms of accommodating different views and opinions. As while a broad array of philosophies and cosmologies can bring a rich sense of diversity and vibrancy to a Collective as a whole, there can often be a limit to how much we can truly open up around people who hold a number of ideas that are diametrically opposed to our own.

And seeing as one of the primary intentions of forming Collectives is to help us move beyond late stage capitalism, whilst simultaneously tackling climate change, environmental degradation and the long list of social injustices and inequities we now face as a species, the politics of each Collective are envisioned to lean towards the progressive end of the spectrum.

32. Is it possible to be part of more than one Collective at a time?

Yes it's definitely possible, however it comes down to a question of personal preference and the amount of time and energy people wish to invest in cultivating community in their life. Participating in each Collective will come with its own unique set of commitments and responsibilities, so it will be up to each individual to decide how many different mutual aid communities they can realistically and meaningfully engage with at once.

33. What are some examples of the kinds of working groups that might form within a Collective?

- **Activism & Advocacy Groups** - To help organise action towards a particular cause.

- **Admissions Groups** - To manage the welcoming in of new members.

- **Conflict Resolution Groups** - To help people peacefully overcome their differences.

- **Counselling/Therapy Groups** - For people to turn to when they need physical and mental health support.

- **Gathering Groups** - To help coordinate the Collective Gatherings.

- **Musical Orchestrators** - To help create a thriving culture of musical collaboration within the Collective

- **Online Moderators Groups** - To help oversee the online components of group communication.

- **Pod Groups** - To assist with the formation of Pods within the Collective

- **Social Enterprise Groups** - To support others in launching and incubating meaningful new projects and business ventures.

- **Structure Groups** - To help oversee the function of the whole Collective. They might be made up of one representative from each other working group.

34. Is there a particular methodology for resolving conflicts within a Collective?

Every community is bound to have a series of conflicts and disagreements that arise along the way. Figuring out how to gracefully navigate these moments with patience and compassion whilst effectively expressing our anger and frustration is one of greatest learning opportunities that participating in Collectives can provide us.

While every Collective will settle on it's own particular process for resolving conflict, a useful template might include:

- Starting out by making sure that every one in the Collective has a shared understanding of the communities conflict resolution processes and that they have agreed to follow the steps together when ever necessary. Also ensuring that everyone knows which resources and what kind of support is available and how to access them.

- Then, if there is a disagreement, first encouraging people to try and resolve the issue between themselves through one to one conversation.

- If a one to one exchange doesn't resolve the issue, or if someone feels unsafe around the idea of such an encounter, then each person may wish to invite a friend from within the Collective to come along and assist in creating the right conditions for reconciliation.

- Beyond this, having a Conflict Resolution Working Group that is made up of some of the more experienced mediators within the Collective (with as wide a spectrum of demographics as possible) can also be hugely beneficial. Such a group can provide advice and support when ever required and also directly assist in helping to resolve conflict when necessary.

35. What happens if someone in a Collective continually violates the rules or guidelines of the group?

Each Collective will decide on their own method for dealing with such a scenario. But one approach is to empower a particular working group with the ability to remove people from the Collective if they repeatedly violate the values and guidelines of the group. The principles of Restorative Justice can also be applied in these situations, which is based on the notion of creating spaces where all stakeholders involved in a particular incident can come together to best determine ways to repair any damage that has been done and then hopefully transform their behaviours and actions going forward.

36. How might Collectives help to counteract the racism that is endemic to modern society?

There are a number of ways that Collectives can help to turn the tide against racism. A good place to start is to cultivate an ongoing culture of learning around the history of racism as well as an ever increasing group awareness of the various ways it manifests overtly and covertly across society today. And it's critical that everyone in the Collective sees it as their shared responsibility to further this kind of work, as people of colour should not be relied upon to have to kickstart and oversee such a process.

Collectives can also act as test beds for actively embodying the principles of racial equity in their decision making processes. Although considering the long history of intense racial trauma that so many BIPOC have had to endure, and the ongoing racial injustice still present in the world today, addressing these dynamics within community may not always be such a smooth or straight forward process. But it remains a critically important task that will require a keen and ongoing awareness of how racial power dynamics and the hangover of generations of systemic racism might subtly manifest and unfold in the Collective context.

A similar awareness and process of ongoing education will also be required around the issue of sexism and in regards to any discrimination towards those of a particular sexual orientation or gender identity. The task for each Collective will be to create a healthy balance of understanding and power between each of the different perspectives, worldview and identities included within the group.

37. Is there a minimum level of engagement required to stay a part of a Collective?

Each Collective will set its own guidelines in relation to this, but it's likely that some minimum level of engagement will be required from each member within the group. This is due to the fact that it can be difficult to continue building trust and cohesion as a community if certain members are regularly absent or simply don't participate.

38. How can Collectives cater to the needs and desires of Introverts & Highly Sensitive People?

In our modern culture many social settings and contexts are not designed for the introverts and Highly Sensitive People (HSP) amongst us. For those unfamiliar with the concept of HSP's, the psychologist Elaine Aron published a book in 1996 outlining the concept that a small percentage of the population are what she labelled Highly Sensitive People, in that they experience a high degree of what has come to be known as sensory processing sensitivity.[48] Essentially these individuals are highly attuned to their surrounding environment. There are a number of ways that Collectives can ensure Introverts and HSP's feel welcomed, included and valued by the community. The creation of Pods and other small groups that meet up to partake in activities play a big part in this, as does holding events that are more peaceful or less 'high energy' in nature. But perhaps the most fundamental aspect is simply acknowledging that there are Introverts and HSP's within the Collective and ensuring that they feel recognised, understood and represented in any decision making processes.

* * *

39. Will there be whole families in each Collective? Should I invite my Mum along too?

As long as each individual aligns with the values of the community then it's definitely possible to have various generations of the same family participating in a Collective. In the years to come it will be interesting to observe whether most individuals prefer to either bond together or seperate out their Collective identity and experience from their familial one. We shall see over time how this particular dynamic plays out and discover which approach tends to lead to the healthiest Collective culture.

40. What role will ritual play in the Collective Experience?

Rituals are an integral part of human culture and can play an important role in rejuvenating our sense of psychological well being. Participating in Collectives can provide us with an opportunity to re-introduce the use of ritual into our lives in order to celebrate what we feel to be sacred, as well as steady and empower us through times of transition. Some examples of the kind of rituals that can emerge within a Collective context include:

- A welcoming in of new members as well as an honouring of those that leave the group.

- A practice of everyone writing each other anonymous notes of gratitude and appreciation at the annual Gathering.
- Meeting together on the solstices and equinoxes to set new goals as individuals and as a Collective.

Appendix II.
Where To Learn More

If you're interested in learning more about weaving mutual aid communities then I recommend the following resources:

- Richard Bartletts Microsolidarity Proposal as well as The Microsolidarity Loomio Group.
- The Community Canvas website (www.community-canvas.org).
- The Community Builders Facebook Group.
- The website of Enspiral, a mutual aid community based in New Zealand (www.enspiral.com).
- Being The Change, a book by Terry Patten, Siobhan McClory & Kristin Nauth.
- A Different Drum, a book by M. Scott Peck.

And for a further exploration of the intersection between the existential threats we face as a species, community building and the movement towards a new societal narrative, I recommend this list of resources:

- Bildung by Lene Rachel Anderson.
- Sand Talk By Tyson Yunkaporta.
- The Listening Society & The Nordic Ideaology by Hanzi Frienacht.
- Out Of The Wreckage by George Monbiot.
- These Wilds Beyond Our Fences by Bayo Akomolafe.

- How Soon Is Now by Daniel Pinchbeck.

- Tribe by Sebastian Junger.

- Social Ecology & Communalism by Murray Bookchin.

- Beyond Civilisation by Daniel Quinn.

- The Revolution Now speech by Angela Davis at the CCCB in 2017.

Appendix III.
Collective Bonding Projects

Here are some examples of the kinds of projects that can unfold in a Collective context. Each of them is intended to generate a deep sense of cohesion and belonging between members of a community, whilst also encouraging personal development, social change and just generally being fun to participate in.

The Origins Story Project

This project is involves inviting each person in a Collective to share their Origins Story with the rest of the group. The Origins Story idea is borrowed from the world of comic books and refers to the stories that reveal the how the main characters become heroes in the first place. Using just twelve photos and a small number of words to describe them, each month a different community member is invited to post in an online community space and tell the story of how they became the multifaceted 'hero' they are today. Often there are so many wonderful people in our communities that we simply don't have enough time to meet up in person and share the intricacies of where we've come from, so the Origins Story project is a great way to deepen our shared understanding of how we came to be. It also provides an opportunity for the participant to self author their own story and to frame their history the way they wish to, which can be a surprisingly transformative and therapeutic process to undertake.

The Hatchery

The Hatchery is a seven week program designed to help members of a Collective incubate or launch new Social Enterprises. The format is simple, after an introductory session, each of the remaining six weeks are dedicated to one member of the group. Each week a different participant shares about a new idea or an existing project which they wish to either launch or further evolve. They then receive coaching, feedback and advice from the other participants, as well as any other experienced entrepreneurs in the Collective who are happy to donate their time. This format can also be applied to running Case Clinics, which is a methodology with similar aims to the Hatchery which emerged from the management methodology Theory U.

Solstice Goals

The Solstice Goals project involves inviting members of a Collective to meet together on all four of the Solstices and Equinoxes in order set their goals and intentions for the three months ahead. The idea is to help each other stay on track with achieving our dreams and to support each other to remain healthy and balanced while we do it. Breakout sessions held during the event provide an opportunity to help coach each other in small groups, after which everyone is then invited (but not obliged) to publicly state what it is they are aiming for in the months ahead. There is also a chance to celebrate successes and commiserate about any frustrations people experienced while trying to reach their goals in the previous three months. It's a practice that also serves as invitation for the community to come together and find a moment of Collective stillness, to recognise the changing of the seasons and to reflect upon everything that is happening our lives.

The Creative Boost

The Creative Boost is a project designed to support the artists, writers, comedians, poets, musicians and other kinds of performance artists within the group. Every month or a two, a different Collective member that falls into one of these categories (be they professional or amateur) is chosen. They then share with the wider community a list of ways that they can be supported by the group that will help to boost them in their creative endeavours. This might involve having people like a social media page, leave a review online or buy an album or a book. The rest of the Collective are then invited to choose one of the 'boosting methods' and flood the particular artist with a sense of appreciation and support.

The Annual Meme Contest

The Annual Meme contest invites everyone in the Collective to create their own meme around a particular subject or topic and then post it in an online community space. The rest of the community then votes on which one they like the best, different categories can involve 'most creative' and 'most funny but true'. Such meme contests can also serve as a means for the Collective to make fun of itself and point towards any shadow elements that are not often openly discussed within the community.

The Grand Eco Challenge

Each year, during one particular month, everyone in the Collective can be invited to participate together in a Grand Eco challenge. This involves each person taking stock of how their lifestyle choices impact the surrounding ecology. Participants then make a commitment to make relevant changes in their lifestyle. Annual themes might include removing or reducing animal products from our diets, composting at home, increasing the use of bicycles or cutting out the use of plastic in our live. The motivation to follow through on the behaviour change comes from the fact that there is a group commitment to doing it together. It's a process that can be made more fun and enjoyable by encouraging everyone to post photos and share stories along the way of what did and didn't work, and by celebrating the victories each person has along the way.

Notes

1. Tyson Yunkaporta, *Sand Talk*, Melbourne: Text Publishing, 2019, Pg. 3.

2. The words of Carl Rogers from the the documentary film *Journey Into The Self*, Produced by Bill Mcgaw, 1968.

3. Waldo Noesta, *Emergence of the Contemplative Shaman- Part One*, nondualmedia.org, 23/3/2017.

4. Miller McPherson, Lynn Smith-Lovin and Matthew E. Brashears *American Sociological Review* Vol. 71, No. 3, June 2006, Pg. 353-375.

5. WRVS Report, *Loneliness Amongst Older People & The Impact Of Family Connections*, Cardiff, 2012.

6. Mental Health Foundation Report, *The Lonely Society?*, London, 2010.

7. National Academies of Sciences, Engineering, and Medicine, *Social Isolation and Loneliness in Older Adults: Opportunities for the Health Care System.* Washington, DC, 2020.

8. Norimitsu Onishi, *A Generation in Japan Faces a Lonely Death*, New York Times, 30/11/2017.

9. Johnathon Cott, *The Cosmos: An Interview With Carl Sagan*, Rolling Stone Magazine, 25/121980.

10. BBC Future, *Are We On The Road To Civilisation Collapse?*, BBC.com, 2019.

11. Ronald Wright, *Civilization Is A Pyramid Scheme by Ronald Wright*, Globe And Mail, 2000.

12. Jared Diamond, *Collapse: How Societies Choose to Fail or Survive*, Penguin Books, 2011, Pg. 509.

13.   Jeremy Lent, *Our Actions Create The Future: A Response To Jem Bendell*, mahb.stanford.edu, 15/3/2019.

14.   George Monbiot, *Out Of The Wreckage*, Verso, 2017, Pg. 1.

15.   Presentation by Terence McKenna, *Culture & Ideology Are Not Your Friends*, Presented at the Whole Life Expo, Denver, April 1999.

16.   Noam Chomsky, *Profit Over People*, Seven Stories Press: New York, 1999.

17.   Douglas Keay, *Aids, Education & The Year 2000* (An interview with Margeret Thatcher), Women's Own Magazine, 1987.

18.   Presentation by Yannis Varoufakis, *Live at Politics & Prose Talk*, New York, 5/10/18.

19.   Primo Levi, *The Black Hole Of Auschwitz*, Chapter 12, Cambridge, Polity Press, 2002.

20.   Interview with Frank Zappa, Keyboard Magazine, San Bruno, California, 1987.

21.   John Perkins, *Confessions Of An Economic Hitman*, Berrett-Koehler Publishers, Oakland California, 2004.

22.   Monika A Bauer, James E B Wilkie, Jung K Kim, Galen V Bodenhausen, *Cuing consumerism: situational materialism undermines personal and social well-being*, Psychological Sciences Journal, 2012,

23.   Alnoor Ladha & Martin Kirk, *Capitalism Is Just A Story And Other Dangerous Thoughts, Part 1*, Occupy.com, 3/19/2015.

24.   Michael Catalano, *The Prospect of Designer Babies: Is it Inevitable?*, PIT Journal, Cycle 3, 2012.

25. Speech, Richard Flanagan: 'Will you stand with me, will you go to jail with me', Adani mine rally, 5 May 2019, Canberra, Australia

26. Original source unknown, though widely attributed to the anthropologist Margeret Mead.

27. See Hanzi Frienachts model of Effective Value Memes in the Listening Society for an explanation of one approach to identifying these different levels of cultural code.

28. M. Scott Peck, The Different Drum: Community Making and Peace, Simon and Schuster, 2010, Pg. 59.

29. Television interview of Noam Chomsky by Bill Moyer on the show A World Of Ideas, PBS, 1988.

30. Hanzi Frienacht, *The Listening Society*, Chapter 2 Crisis Revolution - Hackers, Hipsters & Hippies, MetaModerna ApS, 2017.

31. M. Scott Peck, The Different Drum: Community Making and Peace, Simon and Schuster, 2010, Pg. 165.

32. Bruce Parry, www.tawai.earth/essay-from-bruce-parry.

33. Brian Duffy, *How Burning Man and Festival Culture Make Change Personal*, realitysandwich.com, 3/9/2014.

34. L. Steven Sieden, *A Fuller View - Buckminster Fuller's Vision of Hope and Abundance For All*, Divine Arts Media, 2011, Pg. 358.

35. Bessel Van Der Kolk, *The Body Keeps The Score*, Penguin Books, 2014.

36. Hanzi Freinacht, *The Painful Dance Between (In)dividuation and Differentiation*, metamoderna.org, 21/2/2020.

37. Dieter Duhm, *Terra Nova: Global Revolution & The Healing Of Love*, Verlag Meiga, 2015.

38. Charles Tebbet's Parts Process & Carl Jung's theory of Archetypes are two examples of such psychological models.

39. Anyone experiencing persistent mental health issues should be encouraged to seek out the assistance of a trained mental health practitioner.

40. Richard D. Bartlett, microsolidarity.cc/articles, 2018-2020.

41. M. Scott Peck, The Different Drum: Community Making and Peace, Simon and Schuster, 2010, Pg. 165.

42. Robin Dunbar, *How Many Friends Does One Person Need*, Harvard University Press, 2011.

43. Anthony Charuvastra & Marylene Cloitre, *Social Bonds and Posttraumatic Stress Disorder*, Annual Review of Psychology, Vol. 59, Pg. 301-328, Jan 2008.

44. Paul Hawken's Commencement Address to the Class of 2009, University Of Portland, 3/5/2009.

45. Richard D. Bartlett, *How To Weave Social Fabric, 3 Essential Pillars For a New Mutual Aid Community*, medium.com, 22/1/2020.

46. Hanzi Freinacht, Nordic Ideology, Metamoderna ApS, 2019, Kindle location 1908.

47. Hanzi Freinacht, Nordic Ideology, Metamoderna ApS, 2019, Kindle location 2815.

48. Elaine Aron, *The Highly Sensitive Person*, Broadway Book, 1997.

About The Author

Joe Lightfoot is a writer and weaver of community.

He focuses on the overlap between the cultivation of new kinds of mutual aid community, the emergence of a regenerative planetary culture and the inner journey of transformation that is required for each of us to become truly Communal Creatures.

The question that inspires him the most is how best we can step into a paradigm that combines the wisdom of Organic Society with the intelligence of the Modern World. He is often found in either Melbourne, Australia or Chiang Mai, Thailand.

You can reach him online at www.joelightfoot.org.